Market day, Samarkand. Photo by S.M. Dudin, 1902.

Mountain road, Caucasus, late 19th century.

View of Tbilisi on the Kura River, with Zion Cathedral, late 19th century.

(Russian Museum of Ethnography)

Facing West

Oriental Jews of Central Asia and the Caucasus

Waanders Uitgevers, Zwolle
Joods Historisch Museum, Amsterdam
Russian Museum of Ethnography, St Petersburg

Contents

previous pages
Young Jewish man, Bukhara, 1890-1910.
Photo by D.I. Ermakov.
(Russian Museum of Ethnography)

Jewish quarter, Samarkand, 1933.
(Indigenous Jewish Museum Collection,
Municipal Museum, Samarkand)
Synagogue, Kuba, early 20th century.
(Beth Hatefutsoth Photo Archive)
Jewish quarter in Tskhinvali, 1934.
(Beth Hatefutsoth Photo Archive)

above
Wealthy Jewish family, Tbilisi, early 20th
century.
(Beth Hatefutsoth Photo Archive, courtesy of
M. Gani, Ramat Gan, S. Miller Tel Aviv)

5   Foreword

7   The Eastern Jewish Communities of the Former USSR
    Valery Dymshits

33 Central Asian Jewish Costume
    Tatjana Emelyanenko

63 Catalogue Central Asia

75 Jews of the Caucasus
    Vladimir Dmitriev

107 Catalogue Caucasus, Mountain Jews

120 Catalogue Caucasus, Georgia

Foreword

Prof. I. Dubov
Russian Museum of Ethnography, St Petersburg
Judith C.E. Belinfante
Jewish Historical Museum, Amsterdam

On 10 September 1996 the exhibition of the An-sky collection opened in the Russian Museum of Ethnography in St Petersburg. It was the end of a successful tour that had started in the Jewish Historical Museum in Amsterdam in 1992, of a collection that had acquired almost legendary status. In the intervening years the show had visited Cologne, Frankfurt, Jerusalem, New York and St Petersburg, Florida.

That tour was the first joint project of our two institutions. And it was not long after the opening of the An-sky exhibition in Amsterdam that preparations began for a second joint project: an exhibition of part of the Sephardi collection of the Russian Museum of Ethnography, a collection featuring objects from Central Asia, the Caucasus and the Crimea. *Facing West. Oriental Jews of Central Asia and the Caucasus* highlights a little-known Jewish world, whose origins stretch far back, perhaps more than two millennia. A Jewish world in which Persia formed the central focus. A Jewish world in which far-reaching integration into the surrounding society did not lead to assimilation. And a Jewish world that only began to adapt to the traditions of European Jewry after coming into contact with Sephardi Jews in the eighteenth century. The Jewish world of the Orient, in whose synagogues the direction of Jerusalem is indicated by the Ark at the western wall.

After a first exploratory investigation of the collection it was decided to set the Crimean objects aside for a separate project. This catalogue therefore focuses on work on objects from Central Asia and the Caucasus and represents the first publication of descriptions and research articles.

In Russia, the project was coordinated by our friend and highly professional colleague Dr Ludmila Uritskaya, chief curator. In addition to contributions from the highly proficient and expert curators of the Russian Museum of Ethnography Dr Vladimir Dmitriev and Dr Tatjana Emelyanenko, this is also the first joint project with the St Petersburg Jewish University and the Israeli Centre for Jewish Art in Jerusalem. Thanks to their expeditions into areas now regularly torn apart by civil war, Dr Valery Dymshits and Dr Aliza Cohen have managed to bring much to light which would otherwise have been lost. In Amsterdam Hetty Berg coordinated the editing of the texts, as well as the progress of the exhibition. And once again Alla Geller was proved an indispensable intermediary between Holland and Russia. We thank all those involved for the tremendous effort and the enthusiasm with which, sometimes under intense pressure, they did their work.

The exhibition and catalogue could not have been achieved without the support of the Friends of the Jewish Historical Museum, Stichting Charity, The Hague, Prins Bernhard Fonds/Oost Europa Fonds, Stichting The Zimet Foundation, WRC2 Fonds in Kortenhoef, Prof.dr. Herman Musaph Fonds, KLM Royal Dutch Airlines and private individuals.
We are grateful to all those concerned.

In this premiere presentation, the museum showcases an Oriental Jewish world which, without perhaps the familiarity of the An-sky collection, nevertheless represents a valued part of that colourful, varied Jewish culture. We hope that this little-known Jewish world will find its way into the museums of Europe, Israel and America.

Editor's note

Because of the diversity of the languages referred to in this book, various systems of transliteration have been employed. Where available, geographical names are borrowed from the Times Atlas of the World.

Each part of the catalogue section opens with an outline of the history and ethnography of the Jews of the area concerned.
In 1992-1997, the St Petersburg Jewish University and the Centre for Jewish Art at Hebrew University in Jerusalem organised a series of joint historical and ethnographical expeditions to study the Bukharan, Mountain and Georgian Jews.

The author, Valery Dymshits visited numerous Jewish communities in the Caucasus and Central Asia. This review is based on his personal impressions as well as on summarised literary data.

Information about each catalogue item is presented in the following order: inventory number, title and description, including materials, size, place and date of production, place and date of usage and how the item was acquired.

Numbers in the colour illustration captions refer to items in the Jewish collections only.

The Eastern Jewish Communities of the Former USSR

Valery Dymshits, St Petersburg Jewish University

> *... he settled them in Halah, in Habor,*
> *on the river Gozan, and in the Median cities.*
> (2 Kings 17:6)

The Jews of the former Soviet Union, the Russian Jews as they are known in the West, are generally defined as the Russian-speaking descendants of the former inhabitants of the Pale of Settlement: part of what was once a vast Ashkenazi Diaspora. But there are many smaller groups of Jews, each with their own language, traditions and history, living in the former Soviet regions: the Bukharan Jews, Mountain Jews, Georgian Jews, Crimean Jews, Kurdistan Jews, or Lakhlukhs, Persian Jews (Ironi) and the Gerim, descendants of Russian peasants who converted to Judaism some two hundred years ago.

Most important (and numerous) are the first three: the Tajik-speaking Bukharan Jews of Central Asia, the Tat-speaking Mountain Jews of Eastern Caucasia and the Georgian-speaking Jews of Georgia. Each has its own specific characteristics; but they also have much in common. In the following description of the Eastern Jewish communities of the former Soviet Union these similarities are compared against the historical and cultural background.

To a scholar and an outsider, the most obvious similarity is that all these Jewish communities form pockets of 'internal aliens' within the larger Ashkenazi world. Each presents a mirror, posing questions about Jewish identity and inviting a re-examination of the history and diversity of the Jewish world.

One particular fact about all these Jewish communities makes them especially interesting: without exaggeration, they are probably the only Jewish communities of the former Soviet Union that have continued to live in the same areas. In the rest of the country, the hundred years from 1880 to 1980 was not only a period of catastrophe, it was also a period of mass Jewish migration. Social change, war and revolution scattered most of the Jewish population. And it was not just Ashkenazim who were affected; the Jews of the Islamic world were affected by change as well. Whether these migrations were voluntary or forced, whether the migrants were escaping, emigrating, repatriating or moving from shtetl to city – today most of the Jewish communities are no longer where they were a hundred years ago. In fact, nowadays much of Jewish ethnography is more like paleoethnography.

In contrast, the Jews of the Caucasus and Central Asia still live where they once formed separate ethnic groups. They are a unique survival. Naturally, the wave of Soviet Jewish emigration and the population movements of the post-

Soviet era have had their effect on these communities. Nevertheless, more than any other Jewish group, they offer a unique source for historical and ethnic study. It is still possible to examine the community and family structure on site, and to record the traditions, rituals, beliefs and folklore.

COMMON BACKGROUND AND RELIGIOUS LIFE

Ever since Jews started leaving the Holy Land there have been two potential migration routes: east and west. Historically, the first diaspora was in Babylon, to the east. Its origins lay in the deportation of the Jewish population from Israel by the Assyrians, and from Judah by the Babylonians. In successive centuries the Babylonian community was augmented by waves of refugees, especially after the destruction of the Second Temple in 70 CE. Throughout the first millennium CE the Babylonian Diaspora remained the most important Jewish community and the centre of spiritual development, as the Babylonian Talmud itself testifies.

Known as the Babylonian community, this centre of Jewish life continued through the Achaemenid, Parthian, and Sassanid periods, and eventually also the Caliphate, generating a host of smaller communities and sub-ethnic Jewish groups in Asia. This was a result of the secondary dispersal of the Babylonian Diaspora. While the Georgian Jewish community's roots lie so far in the past that it is no longer possible to establish its origins with any certainty, the Mountain Jews and the Bukharan community are clearly descended from Persian Jews whose ancestors first arrived in Persia from Mesopotamia. They maintained their connections with Persian Jewry for centuries. Emigration of Jews from Persia to Georgia continued throughout the Middle Ages, and to Eastern Caucasia and Central Asia until the eighteenth and nineteenth centuries. There is considerable evidence of this connection with Persia: from the forms of religious objects to the traditional trades of Bukharan and Georgian Jews, such as weaving and cloth dyeing. The direction their ancestors took is still reflected in their synagogues: the Ark – the *Aron ha-kodesh* or *Hekhal* – is at the western wall. Unlike Ashkenazim, Bukharan, Mountain and Georgian Jews build their synagogues facing west. A curious illustration of this inbuilt historical awareness is the Ashkenazi synagogue and that of the Mountain Jews in Baku. They are on adjoining streets, but the former faces east, and the latter west, while Jerusalem is actually to the southwest.

Clearly, their common background accounts for much that is similar in the Central Asian and Caucasian communities. But ethnographically there is a considerable resemblance to the local populations. This includes the social structure of the communities, housing, food (apart from *kashrut*, of course), dress, art, folklore, music and musical instruments, rituals, rites, beliefs and superstitions, as well as language. This is best illustrated with the Georgian Jews, almost the only group in the Jewish Diaspora that has not developed its own language or dialect; they speak pure Georgian, each community sharing the dialect of its area. An outsider would find it difficult to distinguish a Jew of this area from the ethnic majority.

Since Rabbi Gershom's prohibition of polygamy did not affect the Eastern communities, many Bukharan Jewish men had two wives, while among Mountain Jews three wives was fairly common. It was usual for the Jews of Central Asia and the Caucasus to have large families, with three or four generations of relatives living together. And several families would trace their origins to a common ancestor to form a kind of clan. As Jews migrated in the eighteenth and nineteenth centuries from old to new communities this common background gained added significance in their internal organisation. The largest Jewish settlement, the Kuba district of Krasnaya Sloboda, is divided into sections – *mahallas* – named after the villages from which the ancestors of the present inhabitants came. A Bukharan Jew's social status is still largely determined by the ancestral birthplace. Finally, the ultimate form of the Jewish community structure was, and to an extent still is, the autonomous Jewish quarter.

These communities have one other feature in common. They all used to have their own religious rituals and manuscripts. The rituals of the Georgian and the Mountain Jews have not been preserved or recorded. Those of the Bukharan Jews survive in a single manuscript which describes the so-called

In the synagogue, Samarkand, 1932.
(Indigenous Jewish Museum Collection, Municipal Museum, Samarkand)

nusah khorasan (Khorasan is a northeastern province of Iran). The austerity of religious life led to the import of printed books from Italy (Livorno, Venice) and the Holy Land, and the gradual substitution of the local liturgy with Sephardic traditions, the so-called *nusah sepharad*, since manuscript books could not compete with cheaper printed editions. It is not known when exactly the Jews of the Caucasus adopted the Sephardi liturgy, probably it was in the late sixteenth and early seventeenth centuries. Books of this period, printed in Venice, have been preserved in one of the synagogues of the Mountain Jews of Kuba. In 1792 a Moroccan-born fund raiser, Rabbi Joseph Mamon Maghribi, arrived in Bukhara from Safed. Seeing the deplorable state of the community, he decided to stay in Bukhara. It was Joseph Mamon who persuaded the Bukharan Jews to adopt the Sephardi liturgy. His efforts resulted in a revival of religious life, he founded a *yeshiva* in Bukhara and Sephardi prayerbooks, mostly published in Italy, began to arrive in Central Asia. In the conventional division of the Jewish world into Ashkenazim and Sephardim, the communities of Central Asia and Caucasia, like the other Eastern communities, therefore fall within the Sephardi category.

Religious life in Central Asia and the Caucasus had its own unique structure. Religious education was available only to community officials, the *hakhamim*. A *hakham* combined the functions of rabbi, *shohet*, *mohel*, *melamed* and *hazzan*. His principal responsibility was to attend to the practical needs of the community, such as *shehitah*. Among the Mountain Jews a *shohet* was also a rabbi. Synagogues generally had elementary schools, *heders*, but there was hardly anything approaching the Eastern European *yeshiva*.

Jewish spiritual life in the Caucasus and Central Asia had never been intense; the only literary heritage of the Georgian community is a small corpus of *responsa*. Bukharan Jews composed a number of liturgical hymns, *piyyutim*, imitating the popular Sephardi style of the Cabbalist and mystic Israel Nagera of Safed (1546-1625). Apart from Hebrew verse, Bukharan Jews also composed poems in the Bukharan Jewish dialect, taking Jewish themes and imitating classical Persian poetry. At the turn of the seventeenth and eighteenth centuries, a school of poetry led by Joseph ben Isaac (d. 1755), known as Yusuf Yehudy (Joseph the Jew), flourished in Bukhara. In the early nineteenth century the poet Ibrahim ibn Abi-l-Khair wrote a verse on the martyrdom of Khudaidad the Jew, who preferred death rather than convert to Islam.

Among the Mountain Jews, several *piyyutim*, as well as Cabalistic and halakhic pieces, appeared in the seventeenth and eighteenth centuries. The names are recorded of the liturgical poet Elishah ben Samuel and scholar Gershon Lala ben Moses Naqdi, who wrote commentaries on Maimonides' *Mishneh Torah*. Numerous folklore pieces also exist, including epic poems, composed by Mountain Jews in the Tat language. Nevertheless, even this humble literary tradition had declined by the early nineteenth century, as the crisis among the Eastern Jewish communities worsened.

Extensive contacts with the Ashkenazi world signalled an improvement in the religious life of the Eastern communities. These only began, however, in the early nineteenth century. It is well known, for example, when the first contacts occurred with the Bukharan Jews. In 1802 a Bukharan Jew named Benjamin wrote a letter in Hebrew to the Jewish community of the town of Shklov, in Byelorussia, asking a number of questions about Jewish life in Russia. He had learned of their existence from Moslem merchants who had been to Russian fairs. He was interested in the trading opportunities in Russia for Bukharan Jewish merchants, and he wondered whether the Russian Jews were descended from the Ten Lost Tribes of Israel.

Contacts between Ashkenazim and so-called indigenous Jews increased when Central Asia and the Caucasus were incorporated into Russia. Not that these contacts were ever either intense or smooth: the language barrier, as well as the different religious practices and lifestyles presented considerable obstacles. Local Jews could hardly tell the difference between Ashkenazim and ordinary Russians, while for European Jews the locals were just another group of primitive Asians.

Relations were particularly strained in the Eastern Caucasus, where Ashkenazi Jews arrived in large numbers in the late nineteenth century. European Jews called the local Jews 'bulls', a reference to their lack of education. Mountain Jews retorted with claims that the Ashkenazim were not orthodox, and by refusing to support the activities of the SPE, the society for promotion of education among Russian Jews. A Mountain Jewish saying held that 'it's better to stab an Ashkenazi in the back of the head, than in the throat', this more painful death reflecting a nadir in intercommunal relations.

By the late nineteenth century, the Ashkenazi community of Georgia was almost twice the size of the Georgian Jewish community. Their relations were not always friendly either. When, in the late 1890s, the authorities appointed the Ashkenazi rabbi of Tbilisi to be the city's chief rabbi, the Georgian Jews refused to accept the decision.

But despite the conflicts, these contacts with Russian Jews ended the isolation of Central Asian and Caucasian Jews from the rest of the Jewish world. Young people were now able to look for an education in European Russia, in the famous Lithuanian *yeshivas*. Religious publications from Vilna, Warsaw and elsewhere became available (no Jewish publishing industry of any note was ever established in Central Asia or the Caucasus). Eventually, rabbis trained in the Ashkenazi religious tradition were appointed to the Eastern Jewish communities.

While Bukharan Jews looked to the Sephardi community of Jerusalem, the Jews of the Caucasus fell increasingly under the influence of the Ashkenazi world. The story of Rabbi Avraham Khvoles (1857-1931) who was elected chief rabbi of the city of Tskhinvali (South Osetia) in the late 1890s is significant. Khvoles was a Lithuanian, a student of the famous Rabbi I.E. Spector, and the only language he had in common with his congregation was Hebrew - which helped improve the Hebrew skills of Tskhinvali's Jews.

Khvoles opened the first *Talmud Torah* school in Georgia, as well as a Hebrew school for girls. Many of his pupils continued their religious studies in Lithuania. One of Rabbi Khvoles' students was the Georgian Zionist leader Rabbi David Baazov. In the early twentieth century Habad began to penetrate the Georgian communities. By the 1920s Habad rabbis had become so influential in Georgia (especially in Kutaisi, home of the largest community of Georgian Jews) that their debate with the Zionist activists split the Jewish community in the short period of Georgian independence.

Mountain Jews also established contacts with Ashkenazim. A mixed Jewish quarter was established in Baku, with Ashkenazim, Mountain, Georgian and Kurdistani Jews. Increasingly, the rabbis and *shohets* of the Eastern Caucasian communities were educated in Lithuania. One of the first Mountain Jewish writers, the rabbi of the village of Tarka, Rabbi Sherbat Nissim-Oglu, father of the first historian of the Mountain Jews, Ilya Anisimov, studied in Lithuania.

Yet the various contacts between Eastern and European Jews did not result in a merging of the communities: intermarriage was rare. The only exception was the contact between Mountain Jews and Gerim, who followed the Ashkenazi tradition, *nusah ashkenas*, and had a sophisticated religious identity. In 1840s, the Gerim were exiled to the Transcaucasian area. There is still a village called Privolnoye in Southern Azerbaijan, inhabited by Gerim. In the late nineteenth century Mountain Jews began to move to Privolnoye, where they were welcomed by the Gerim. Mountain Jews, altogether some twenty families, were soon assimilated in Privolnoye; this included mixed marriages, for the Gerim regarded marriage with 'natural' Jews as a special honour. It is significant that in the 1940s some fifteen Gerim families moved from the Voroneg region, to the Jewish district of Krasnaya Sloboda in Kuba, in the genuine belief that it would be easier in the uni-national environment of Krasnaya Sloboda to keep to the Jewish precepts. In 1970s the Gerim of Krasnaya Sloboda moved to Israel.

ERETS ISRAEL

Another feature that these Jewish communities have in common is, from the mid-nineteenth century, the steady flow of emigrants to Erets Israel, mostly to Jerusalem, and to their own districts of that city. These settlements, small at first, soon became the spiritual focus of most of the Bukharan, Georgian and Mountain Jews. In fact, it was in Jerusalem that the descendants of the Eastern communities first founded their own religious centres, no longer having to depend on the cultural supervision of Sephardi and Ashkenazi communities.

This is particularly true of the Bukharan Jews. Between 1880 and 1914 over 1,500 Bukharan Jews (around eight per cent of the entire community) moved to Palestine and settled in Jerusalem where a Bukharan Jewish quarter was founded. In fact the area still exists, albeit only in name. The percentage of Bukharan Jews that emigrated to Palestine, compared to other Jewish communities, was one of the highest in the world. A school of Bukharan Jewish writers was established in Jerusalem, led by Rabbi Shimon Hakham (1843-1910); their greatest achievement was the creation of a literary version of their language, based on the Jewish Tajik dialect and the translation of religious and secular Jewish and non-Jewish works into it, as well as the introduction of publishing. Links between Bukharan Jews and the Sephardi community were intensified in Jerusalem. Young men from Central Asia would study in the Sephardi *yeshivas*, while wealthy Jewish merchants would employ Sephardi teachers from Jerusalem to tutor their children in Samarkand and Bukhara.

While their migrations were less extensive, by the beginning of the First World War Mountain and Georgian Jewish communities had been established in Jerusalem, each with a population of around 400. It was in Jerusalem that the spiritual life of the Mountain and the Georgian Jews revived. In the 1880s, Kolel Dagestan and the Georgian Kolel Gurgi (derived from Gurgistan, Turkish for Georgia) were established in Jerusalem. In 1894, shortly after moving to Jerusalem, Sherbat Nissim-Oglu published a Hebrew book on the heritage of the Mountain Jews. In 1877 Rabbi Jacov Kukiashvili published his commentary on the Torah.

While at the turn of the century the Bukharan Jews went to live in Jerusalem for traditional religious reasons, for the Mountain and Georgian Jews their motivation was the Zionist ideal. They became involved in Zionism at an early stage: Mountain Jews took part in the Second Zionist Congress, Georgian Jews joined at the Sixth. It is significant that the first book published in the Judeo-Tat language was a translation of Joseph Sapir's *Zionism*, published in 1908 in Vilna by Asaf Pinhasov. Inevitably, after the establishment of Soviet power in the early 1920s contact between the Jews of Central Asia and Caucasia and Jerusalem ceased.

INTERRELIGIOUS RELATIONS

Caucasia and Central Asia are areas that belong to the cultural nucleus of Eurasia. Jews have lived here since ancient times. It is significant that legend has always identified these Jews as descendants of the Ten Lost Tribes of Israel. Yet once the decline of these communities began in the Late Middle Ages it continued until the nineteenth century, both through forced conversions to Christianity and Islam, and through lack of contact with the rest of the Jewish world.

In the mid-eighteenth and early nineteenth centuries Bukharan Jews were still being forcibly converted to Islam. These and their descendants formed the Chala community (meaning 'belonging nowhere') of clandestine Jews, the Marranos of the East, who had to pretend to keep to the Moslem traditions. The lives of the Chalas were continually threatened by the Emirate authorities. The situation in Bukhara in 1901 was described by Ai-Bibshi Jakubova, a Chala herself, in a letter to the Russian Governor of Syrdar'ya.

'Chalas go to the Mosque as if to pray and generally do everything a Moslem is supposed to do, for they are continually watched by their neighbours. But in their homes, they keep the Sabbath strictly, praying according to the Jewish tradition in the darkness of night [...] If anyone finds and betrays you, you are in trouble: the entire family of an infidel may be hanged; in the old days they were thrown from a high tower and fed to the dogs'.

Chalas were a secluded community: neither Moslems nor Jews would marry them. The remains of the Chala community can still be found in Bukhara. Similar processes occurred in the mid-nineteenth century in Eastern Caucasia. In the days of Imam Shamil in Upper Dagestan, many Mountain Jews were forcibly converted to Islam. Even today Moslems in many mountain villages of Dagestan and Azerbaijan recall their Jewish backgrounds.

Forced conversions resulted in a drastic reduction of the Jewish population throughout the Caucasus, events that can still be traced to this day. During the 1997 expedition we learned from the inhabitants of Krasnaya Sloboda, the Jewish district of Kuba, that some of the residents originally came from the Tat village of Shudukh in the highlands which Jews had abandoned long ago. An eighteenth-century German traveller, Herbert, mentioned Jews living there. When the recent Russian expedition visited the village one of the clans of the Tat, i.e. Moslem, population of Shudukh was found to be called Israili. Members of the clan still remember their ancestor's Jewish background. Until 1946, there had been a Jewish cemetery in the village. It is noteworthy that the Moslem Tats of Shudukh believe the Jews from Krasnaya Sloboda to be their kin and refer to them as such. Clearly, while no date can be established, at some point some of the Jews of Shudukh accepted Islam, and the others had to leave the village and settle in the new Jewish district of Kuba.

Georgian Jews, mostly serfs, were often forced to accept Orthodox Christianity by their owners. A common Georgian surname, Ebreyelidze, indicates that the founder of the family was a converted Jew.

Jewish merchants leaving Bukhara for Kazalinsk (Kazakhstan).
(Russian Museum of Ethnography)

Bukharan Jews, 1890-1910s.
(Russian Museum of Ethnography)

LEGAL POSITION

In the seventeenth to nineteenth centuries these communities came under increasing pressure. In addition to the Omar Conditions, restricting the rights of Jews in Moslem countries, Bukharan and Mountain Jews suffered from growing oppression and humiliation.

Bukharan Jews were forced to live in separate districts, wear a special patch on their clothes, a particular type of hat and use a rope for a belt, not unlike the special clothes Jews were required to wear in mediaeval Germany. While collecting the special Jewish tax, the Moslem official would slap the Jew in the face twice. Apart from regular taxes, Bukhara's Emir regularly imposed extra taxes on the Jewish community. When he lost the war against Russia, he made the Jewish community pay three-quarters of the compensation demanded by the victors from the Emirate. Jews were often imprisoned on false charges, and only released when they agreed to be converted.

Like the Bukharan Jews, the Mountain Jews, who lived under the rule of the minor Moslem feudal lords, endured considerable oppression, as the numerous cases of forced conversion to Islam testify. Besides the regular taxes and *harage* (a special personal tax on non-Moslems in Moslem countries), Jews were forced to do all kinds of humiliating and unpleasant work. A Jew could not ride a horse in the presence of a Moslem, Jews had to supply goods and services to the local ruler free of charge. There was a specific formula for extracting money - a Jew had to pay the Moslem warrior to whom he gave food in his house 'for causing toothache'.

In the cities, Jews were restricted to separate districts alongside the non-Jewish areas: Krasnaya Sloboda was a Jewish district in Kuba, as was Jugutlar in Vartashen. Even in the early twentieth century a Jew venturing outside the settlement risked being maltreated, beaten and robbed. Jewish inequality was also manifest in the prohibition of land ownership. According to the sources, the main occupation of the Jews in the Azerbaijani villages of Vartashen and Mudgi was growing tobacco. Almost all the Jews grew tobacco on land they rented. During the recent expedition field trips the shortage of land in the Jewish settlements and districts was noticeable. Even in Kuba, Vartashen or Madzhalis, Jews barely had enough land for a vegetable garden.

For the Mountain Jews the situation deteriorated in the eighteenth century with the start of a succession of wars between Russia, Turkey and Persia that involved the local feudal lords. The end of many of the Jewish communities came with the thirty-year Caucasian War between the Moslem highlanders and Russia that started in 1830s.

Nevertheless, the Mountain Jews, especially those in highland villages, were probably better off than the Bukharan Jews: the Mountain Jews could wear ordinary Caucasian dress, including the traditional local dagger, they were not forced to wear special garments or any distinctions. The main (and probably the only) feature distinguishing Jews from non-Jewish highlanders was that they had fewer silver ornaments, indicating an inferior status.

Georgian Jews were also treated as pariahs. What set the Georgian Jewish community apart was that the majority were serfs. This is almost unique in Jewish history, for, despite the oppression Jews suffered in most countries, they generally enjoyed personal freedom. Serfdom dates from the fourteenth century. With war and unrest rife, Jews looked for protection, but this came at the price of personal freedom. By the eighteenth century most Georgian Jews were serfs of the tsar, of monasteries or local landlords. Some agricultural serfs owed personal services, some (petty traders, artisans) paid quitrent. Being serfs, Jews could be sold, even presented as a gift. Most Georgian Jews only gained their freedom after the abolition of serfdom in Georgia in 1864.

Well into the nineteenth century, when Central Asia and the Caucasus were incorporated into the Russian Empire, the Jews of these areas were still living in the Dark Ages. It is hardly surprising then, that they welcomed Russian intervention. Despite the anti-Jewish laws, compared to feudal Asia, at least Russia offered legal protection to its indigenous Jews. This, alongside contacts with the better-educated Russian Jews, helped not only to sustain, but to increase the sense of Jewish identity; the result was a revival among the Jewish communities of the Caucasus and Central Asia.

The tsarist authorities distinguished between Russian and indigenous Jews. For the latter, in the early period of Russian dominion in Central Asia and the Caucasus, they were inclined to offer rights equal to those of the other indigenous peoples.

Even before the conquest of Central Asia, Russian laws treated the Bukharan Jews favourably, granting them the right in 1833 to join merchant guilds in areas where Jews were not permitted to reside, and in 1844 allowing them to attend the fairs of Orenburg and Nizhniy Novgorod. Central Asia was conquered by Russia in the 1860s, and most of the territory became the Turkestan governorship – including cities with substantial Jewish populations, such as Samarkand, Tashkent, and those of the Fergana Valley; isolated pockets remained in the Bukharan Emirate and Khivan Khanate, as Russian protectorates. The Turkestan administration, noting the Jewish support for the Russian presence and in an attempt to earn their loyalty, preserved Jewish self-government, granted Jews freedom of religion, the right to own real estate and to engage in commerce on Russian soil. The Jewish subjects of the Bukharan Emir were allowed to purchase Russian citizenship by joining a merchant guild. Because of the mediaeval restrictions still in force inside the Emirate, many Bukharan Jews fled to Russian Turkestan.

Bukharan Jews were better informed about the local market, and immediately competed with the Russian merchants. But in the late 1880s, when they were no longer needed as agents of the Russian economy, the government started to restrict their rights. Bukharan Jews were divided into

Silk traders, Uzbekistan, 1890s.
(Russian Museum of Ethnography)

indigenous Jews of the Turkestan Area (those born in Russian Turkestan before the Russian conquest and their descendants) who retained equal rights with the local population (e.g. the right to purchase and own land); the others, i.e. those born in the Bukharan Emirate, were designated alien Jews and ordered to move into the three border towns of Osh, Kattakurgan and Petro-Alexandrovsk, none of which had Jewish communities of any size. Later, cities with traditional Jewish quarters were added to the list: Samarkand, Kokand, Old Margilan. These became a kind of Central Asian Pale of Settlement. A new attack on Bukharan Jewish rights came in 1909. It was decided to expel to these six towns all Jews who could not prove that their family had resided in Turkestan before the Russian occupation. About 5,000 people were set to be moved under this plan; it was only prevented by the start of the First World War.

In the end, Russia's advance into the Caucasus had little impact on the situation of the Jews, since, being peasants, they remained dependent on their landlords: Mountain Jews as tenants, Georgian Jews as serfs. Nevertheless, the situation had started to change in the late nineteenth century, Jews began to migrate to the cities and spread over the entire Eastern and Northern Caucasus (Mountain Jews) and all of Georgia (Georgian Jews).

Once incorporated into the Russian market, a class of wealthy Jews emerged in Central Asia and the Caucasus. Bukharan Jews played a prominent part in the Central Asian cotton trade and the construction of cotton mills, they established successful business relations with the major Russian textile producers, and sold textiles on the Central Asian market; among them were numerous merchants of the First Guild. In fact the European section of Kokand still features magnificent houses in Art Nouveau style, differing radically from the humble Asian dwellings of the old Jewish quarter. Some of the former belonged to the wealthy Jewish merchants involved in the production and sale of cotton. Thus, 96 of the 256 cotton mills in Russian Turkestan belonged to Jews. And Jews were particularly involved in cotton production and trading in the Fergana Valley.

There were fewer wealthy families among the Mountain Jews. Nevertheless, in the late nineteenth century the first Mountain Jewish millionaires appeared: merchants involved in wine and fishery in Derbent and carpet traders in Kuba and Baku. Some of the Georgian Jews also became wealthy traders.

But despite certain improvements for the Eastern communities, at the turn of the century the majority still lived in poverty. One of the side effects of the development of the market and the advance of the textile industry was the impoverishment of thousands of artisans who lost their traditional trades. Thousands of Bukharan Jews, who had been dyeing fabrics for generations, were now unemployed. Families of the Mountain Jews who made their living growing madder, from which pigment was extracted, or in leather processing were left penniless. These Jews joined the urban poor, becoming artisans, pedlars and porters.

As anti-Semitism grew in the Russian Empire in the late nineteenth century, life for the Jews of Central Asia and Caucasia gradually acquired the added burden of the lies and oppression that Jews suffered all over Russia. The concept of blood libel spread to the region, and there were a number of ritual-murder trials, as well as pogroms.

One pogrom occurred in Central Asia in the Jewish quarter of Osh (Fergana Valley, now part of Kirghizia) following a blood libel. It is interesting to note that this pogrom occurred in September 1911, two months after the Beilis trial had started in Kiev.

Similar events took place in the Caucasus. In 1878 dozens of Jews were arrested in Kuba on a blood libel charge; in 1911 the Jews of the village of Tarka in Dagestan were accused of kidnapping a Moslem baby. Charges of ritual murder led to pogroms in Dagestan as late as the 1920s. Six blood libels occurred in Georgia in the second half of the nineteenth century, a record amount for that period. The most famous was the so-called Kutaisi case (the trial took place in Kutaisi) - nine Jews from the village of Sachkhere were accused of the ritual murder of a Christian girl on the eve of Pesah in 1878. The trial attracted the attention of the entire civilized world. An atrocious pogrom shook Kutaisi in 1895. The blood libel affected the Jews of Dagestan and Georgia deeply. It was still being discussed in the local media in the 1960s.

UNDER THE SOVIETS

Tsarist laws regarding indigenous Jews were relatively mild, so, despite the oppression and numerous blood libels, indigenous Jews remained loyal to Russia. This explains why, during the Civil War, Bukharan and Mountain Jews mistook the struggle of local separatists against the Red Army for a continuation of the Moslem-Russian wars and eagerly supported the Soviets. Seventy per cent of the Red Guard volunteers in Dagestan were Mountain Jews.

It was only in Georgia, where the local social-democrats headed an independent democratic republic in 1918-21, that the situation was any different. Here the Jews supported the national government and responded to the Russian Army occupation of Georgia with mass emigration. About 2,000 Jews left Georgia, mostly for Palestine.

The early 1920s were the last opportunity for *aliyah* before the Soviets closed the doors. Around 300 Mountain Jewish families arrived in Palestine in this period, founding their own district in Tel Aviv. The last Georgian Jews to gain permission to leave the USSR moved to Palestine in 1925. In the late 1920s and early 1930s, Bukharan Jewish *aliyah* continued illegally. Some 4,000 people managed to reach Palestine in this period.

When Soviet power was eventually established, the policy of the authorities towards indigenous Jews was similar to the official policy towards the other Jewish communities of the USSR. While Zionism was suppressed and religious life was reduced to a minimum, Jewish proletarian culture and education were promoted, at least as it was understood by the Soviet authorities. Numerous Jewish-Tajik and Jewish-Tat schools were opened, a number of periodicals were established. Until 1929 Bukharan and Mountain Jews had used the Hebrew

alphabet for publications and education, now it was replaced with the Latin script. In the 1930s societies of Bukharan and Mountain Jewish writers were founded. Although Georgian Jews had no separate language of their own, a system of secular Georgian Jewish education was established. Meanwhile, numerous Jewish clubs, amateur and even professional Jewish theatres (in Derbent and Samarkand) were founded. And in Samarkand an Indigenous Jewish Museum was opened in 1927, while a State Museum of History and Ethnography of Georgian Jews was opened in Tbilisi in 1934; both became prominent centres for cultural studies of the respective communities. In the same period an intelligentsia of Central Asian and Caucasian Jews emerged, with writers, poets, historians and linguists, among them the Bukharan Jewish authors Y. Haimov, N. Fuzailov, B. Kalandarov, the poet Muhib (M. Bachaev), the Mountain Jewish linguist Naftali Anisimov and the Georgian Jewish playwright Herzl Baazov.

In the late 1920s, the Mountain and Georgian Jews, mostly living in rural or semi-rural areas, were incorporated into the kolkhoz collective farm system. An attempt was made to introduce the same system among Bukhara's Jews: several Jewish kolkhozes were founded in Uzbekistan, but because most of the Bukharan Jews lived in cities these attempts failed.

All experiments to improve the cultural and economic lot of the Eastern Jewish communities came to an end in 1938, the same time as a similar fate overtook the Ashkenazim. Under the government's anti-Semitic policies, everything that had been achieved in the previous period was now destroyed. In the years 1936 to 1938 numerous Bukharan, Mountain and Georgian Jewish writers, scientist, artists were sent to the Gulag. Even after Stalin's death there was little opportunity for a revival of cultural life among the Eastern Jewish communities. Two or three books were published in the Tat language in Dagestan; the Tats were considered one of the authentic peoples of Dagestan, although in fact in Dagestan most of the Tat-speaking population are Mountain Jews.

During the Second World War much of the area of Jewish settlement in Central Asia and the Caucasus was never occupied by the Germans so that, unlike the Jews elsewhere in the Soviet Union, these communities were not decimated. The Mountain Jews were an exception, however, along with the rest of the Jewish population many perished in Pyatigorsk, Kislovodsk and the Crimea, where an emigree Mountain Jewish kolkhoz had been founded in the 1920s. Two large Mountain Jewish communities in Northern Caucasia, those of Nal'chik and Groznyy, were lucky to survive the Nazi occupation, for the Germans had not yet decided how to treat this obscure ethnic group. Naturally, men from all the Jewish communities of Central Asia and the Caucasus were enrolled in the Army and many died in combat.

The Second World War had another unforeseen impact on the life of these communities: many Ashkenazi Jews who had fled from Northern Russia and from Poland came to the area. Among them, especially those from Poland, there were many who were observant and who gave a new religious impulse to the Eastern Jewish communities.

Purim parade with Mountain Jews in traditional costume on horseback, Tel Aviv, Israel, 1933.
(Beth Hatefutsoth Photo Archive, courtesy of R. Avshalomov)

Zionist activists, Tbilisi, 1924.
(Jerusalem, Central Zionist Archives)

Bar mitzvah, Samarkand, c. 1930. (Indigenous Jewish Museum Collection, Municipal Museum, Samarkand)

Family at the Seder table, Samarkand. (Indigenous Jewish Museum Collection, Municipal Museum, Samarkand)

In the postwar period, Bukharan, Mountain and Georgian Jews increasingly took up professions. With the closure of the Jewish schools, Russian became the principal cultural medium for Bukharan and Mountain Jews. Generally, a Jew from Central Asia or the Eastern Caucasus would have a better command of Russian than other locals of the same social status. This is not true of the Georgian Jews, however, who had never been divided from their surroundings by a language barrier and were traditionally more involved in Georgian culture.

PRESERVATION OF JEWISH TRADITION

In the Soviet period religious and national activities, especially Jewish activities, were largely prohibited. Nevertheless, assimilation among the Eastern Jewish communities was far less pronounced than among the Ashkenazim. In the preservation of Jewish traditions and Jewish identity, it was the Georgian Jews who were the most successful – paradoxically, since they were historically one of the most assimilated and had not even developed their own language. In the league table of preservation of traditions they were followed by the Bukharan, and finally the Mountain Jews.

Central Asia and Caucasia were areas in which local traditions were more successfully preserved than in the rest of the Soviet Union: the traditional lifestyle, community and family structure, compact accommodation within the Jewish districts and settlements played an important role in preserving the cultural and religious identity of Bukharan, Mountain and Georgian Jews. Another fortunate factor was the failure of the Germans to reach Transcaucasia and Central Asia in the Second World War, so that the Jewish population there was spared. Moreover, religious persecution in Georgia was never as intense as in the rest of the Soviet Union. The educational system of *heders* was maintained in Georgia until the 1970s, on a unofficial, but quasi-legal basis.

Perhaps most unusually, an important aspect of the survival of Jewish traditions was the lower level of educational achievement and prestige compared with the Ashkenazim. Religious education was never replaced by the ambition of success in secular subjects as it had been among most Soviet Ashkenazi Jews.

It was centuries of practice of community life and the preservation of the everyday rituals (orthopractice more than orthodoxy) rather than scholarship that allowed most of the life-cycle rituals (circumcision, bar mitzvah, wedding, burial, commemoration) to continue even after restrictions had been imposed on religious leaders, especially since within the robust clan structure all these events involved large gatherings that in turn helped preserve the system of family and neighbourhood relations.

In the Eastern communities scholarly Judaism – the preserve of a small group of spiritual leaders – existed alongside a popular, domestic Judaism, a mixture of Judaic rituals, local rites and folklore. When the Soviets destroyed the traditional education system, when the rabbis were imprisoned and the synagogues closed, popular Judaism, preserved mostly within the family, became the spiritual base of Central Asian and Caucasian communal life.

All the events surrounding the commemoration and mourning of the dead became especially significant in these communities. For example, in the Jewish *mahalla*, commemorative meals are held almost daily. In addition to the annual remembrance, the family is supposed to provide seventeen commemorative meals within the first year of mourning, inviting a few dozen people on each occasion.

Among the Mountain Jews commemoration of the dead is now the main, if not the only religious activity, replacing all other forms of community life. Many Mountain Jews only know one prayer, the mourner's prayer. The 9th of Av (known locally as Soroni - the day of mourning and commemoration) is for the Mountain Jews, as for many other communities, a day of remembrance, primarily of deceased parents. Recently, at the Jewish cemetery of Krasnaya Sloboda, not only was the entire village present; people came from other cities, Russia, Israel and the USA: several thousand. Professional mourners were weeping at the graves. When asked what the occasion was, most replied that it was the day parents were commemorated. Most of those present had no idea of the original significance of the day as a fast for the destruction of the Temple. Remarkably, considerable sums have been spent in recent years on the upkeep of Krasnaya Sloboda cemetery, but not to support the local Hebrew school. And yet this reverence for the dead is not simply tradition, especially when the opulent modern monuments of Sloboda cemetery are compared with the humble, even austere graves of the previous century.

Everyday religious practice differs from one city or community to the next. Observance of Jewish laws and festivals is far from universal: Georgian Jews are the most religious, least involved in Jewish practice are the Mountain Jews, although none are as secularised as the European Jews of the USSR.

Over the years, Eastern communities have borrowed numerous rites, rituals and superstitions from their non-Jewish neighbours, as well as emulating their use of amulets and keepsakes. While much of Jewish religious tradition has been lost, these folk beliefs and superstitions have survived. They are particularly widespread among the Mountain Jews who regularly adopted non-Jewish rituals.

MATERIAL CULTURE

The material culture of the Eastern communities has survived intact. Because of the minimal difference between Jewish and non-Jewish material cultures in Central Asia and the Caucasus the unique religious objects are of particular interest. Central Asia and Caucasia always had more active synagogues than anywhere else during the Soviet period. Most were closed, however; in fact by 1953 all the synagogues of Georgia were shut and re-opening took considerable effort. Only one of the eleven synagogues of Krasnaya Sloboda, in Kuba, still functioned and only two of the more than twenty were preserved in the Jewish

---

NURSERY RHYME OF THE MOUNTAIN JEWS

This nursery rhyme was dictated and translated from Jewish-Tat into Russian by Ester Gelfand, a teacher of the Hebrew school at Krasnaya Sloboda suburb of Kuba in Azerbaijan (Courtesy of the St Petersburg Jewish University)

Raftum e vishe
Chirum banovshe
Dokundum e shishe
Danorum e kirishe
Raftum e kale kugooj pargo
Huruz bisto urus ne bisto
Ze vini mere huni soht
Hune dorum e zimi
Zimi mere gjndum do...

I went to the woods,
I picked a violet
Put it into a can,
Put the can into a sleigh
Went to the great Tsar's court,
The Russian Tsar was not there, just a rooster.
The rooster pecked me on the nose, it bled.
I gave the blood to the earth,
The earth gave me a grain,
I gave the grain to the mill,
The mill gave me flour,
I put flour into a jar,
The jar gave me dough,
I put the dough into an oven,
The oven gave me mazzah,
I gave mazzah to the rabbi
The rabbi gave me Torah.
I gave Torah to God,
God gave long life to my father and uncle.

Interior of Derbent Great Synagogue, late 19th century. (Beth Hatefutsoth Photo Archive, courtesy of N. Elishayev)

Jewish school, Kuba, c. 1920. (Beth Hatefutsoth Photo Archive)

Vostok quarter. Yet in the 1960s and 1970s every more or less sizable community had an active synagogue. In the early 1970s, 30,000 Bukharan Jews of Central Asia had more than 20 synagogues, 40,000 Jews in Georgia had fourteen synagogues (compared to fifteen active synagogues for the 770,000 Jews of the Russian Federation and eight for a Jewish population in the Ukraine of almost equal size).

Synagogues and the synagogue artifacts in Central Asia and the Caucasus are typical examples of Eastern religious design. Women's galleries are a feature of Georgian synagogues, but not of the synagogues of Bukhara and the Mountain Jews. On the rare occasions women come to synagogue, they stay in the entrance. One or more niches in the western wall contain the Torah scrolls: the *Hekhal*. In the centre of the room is a desk from which the Torah is read: a *tevah*. Some of the synagogue interiors are decorated with wall panels featuring landscapes or geometric patterns; most of the walls and the ceilings are bare, however.

As in Persian synagogues, in Bukhara and Georgia the Torah scroll is kept in a wooden cylindrical or prismatic case upholstered with velvet and decorated with ornamental nails. The Torah is read without being removed from the case, the open scroll being placed vertically on the *tevah*. In some Bukharan communities the case is decorated with a special top, representing the *keter* (Crown of Torah), with special pivots for *rimmonim*. Most Torah cases are made locally, but some are imported from Persia. Mountain Jews, like Ashkenazim, cover the Torah with a cloth and read it placed on the *tevah*.

Silver *rimmonim* are normally decorated with pendants, ornaments and Hebrew inscriptions. Most are Persian in style (a sphere with a crown), except for the Georgian, or rather Tbilisi *rimmonim*, made in the stylized image of the Temple. Different *rimmonim* are kept in the synagogues, including examples from Russia and Europe. The Margilan synagogue has a pair of *rimmonim* from Austro-Hungary, and the synagogue of the Mountain Jews of Baku has a set made in Tbilisi. They are used not only for decorating the Torah scrolls, but for the *tevah*. The pointer for reading the Torah is called a *kulmos*. It is normally a flat piece of silver following the outline of a hand. Cabalistic inscriptions on the *rimmonim* and *kulmos* show that they were also regarded as amulets. All the synagogue artifacts are gifts commemorating relatives, as indicated by the inscriptions.

RECENT DEVELOPMENTS

In recent years two trends have affected the lives of Central Asian and Caucasian Jews: the revival of nationalism and mass emigration. Since the 1970s, one of the main factors in the lives of the Jews has been the struggle for the right to emigrate to Israel. One of the areas in which this struggle was most intense was Georgia. This was based on a long-established Zionist tradition and on a heightened sense of Jewish identity. The famous letter from the eighteen heads of Georgian Jewish families to the UN demanding the right to move to Israel was the first testimony of the Jewish revival in the USSR to reach the outside world. In 1971 the Georgian Jews were granted that right, and in the 1970s around 30,000 of the 43,000 Georgian Jews went on *aliyah*, at least 17 per cent of all the Jews who left the USSR in that period. In the mid-1970s around 12,000 Mountain Jews, and about the same number of Bukharan Jews left for Israel. These communities, unlike those of Georgia, were not dramatically affected by the first wave of *aliyah*, since families have always tended to be large there.

Another factor that has affected the Jewish communities of Central Asia and the Caucasus in recent years is *Perestroika* - which gave everyone the right to travel abroad, as well as to express their ethnic, cultural and religious identity - and the disintegration of the Soviet Union.

Old and new synagogues have revived in the Jewish communities of Central Asia and the Caucasus; Jewish schools, cultural societies, newspapers have been founded. Interest in the history and cultural heritage of these communities has been rekindled. Support from religious, cultural and charitable organizations abroad has flowed in.

Meanwhile, Jews have moved out in increasing numbers, mainly to Israel, Russia and the USA. This is in response to the dramatic deterioration of the economy and of living standards on the margins of the former USSR, even compared to Russia. In many areas, the population has been plunged into poverty and unemployment is rife. At the same time, Central Asia and the Caucasus have become politically unstable and embroiled in ethnic conflict. Georgia and Tajikistan have descended into civil war. Bloody pogroms against the Meschetin Turks have occurred in the Fergana Valley in Uzbekistan; in Azerbaijan it was the Armenians who were victimised and expelled from the country. The continuing military conflict between Armenia and Azerbaijan represents a constant threat with young people regularly being drafted into the Azerbaijani army. Moreover, there is military conflict in Chechnya, and the situation in Dagestan remains critical. Nationalism has left its mark everywhere.

In Central Asia, Moslem fundamentalism has raised its head. A pogrom against Jews, Armenians and Russians, took place in Andizhan (Uzbekistan, Fergana Valley) in 1990. While there were no casualties, it sent Jewish emigration from the Fergana Valley souring. On all the expeditions of the Jewish University of St Petersburg, stories of conflicts between Jews and Uzbeks were constantly heard.

Another factor influencing the rise in emigration is the strong family, clan and neighbourhood bond that unites the members of the Eastern Jewish communities. Once a certain percentage of the community has emigrated (now more than half) the others inevitably follow - and soon.

While there is considerable emigration of indigenous Jews from the margins of the former USSR, the European Jews of the area, once a more numerous group in the cities, have left even faster. This is only natural, all around the former Soviet Union the Russian population is fleeing the peripheral areas - among them the Russian-speaking Ashkenazim. For the first time in years, the Eastern communities once again dominate Jewish life in Central Asia and the Caucasus.

It would be unfair to say that the authorities of the new republics are promoting anti-Jewish policies; on the contrary, in many areas Jews have the protection and support of the authorities. Yet this is obviously not enough to stop the flow of emigration. Several important communities have disappeared over the past years, generally because of the unbearable circumstances in which they found themselves. Others have dwindled dramatically. Bukharan Jewish emigration has been especially rapid. Mountain Jewish communities have declined less quickly, although the effect has been noticeable. Two thousand years of Jewish history in Central Asia and the Caucasus seem to be drawing to a close.

SOURCES

Articles in Jewish encyclopaedias and yearbooks in Hebrew, English and Russian, including one edited by F.A. Brockhaus and I.A. Efron.

BUKHARAN JEWS

1. For a comprehensive bibliography of sources on Bukharan Jews see M. Nosonovsky in *Central Asian Jews in Past and Present*, I.S. Dvorkin (ed.), St Petersburg Jewish University (St Petersburg 1995), p. 270-289. The list contains 225 items. The publication also includes a number of presentations and figures on Bukharan Jews. (In Russian)

2. There are not many works on the language, literature and folklore of Bukharan Jews. Generally, the subject is covered in articles on the Judeo-Persian language, its dialects and Judeo-Persian literature.

3. The principal sources on the history and ethnography of Bukharan Jews include the works of Z. Amitin-Shapiro, among them *Women and Wedding Rituals of Indigeneous Bukharan Jews of Turkestan* (Tashkent 1925); *Sketch on Legal Mores of Central Asian Jews* (Tashkent-Samarkand 1931) and of J. Kalontarov. (In Russian)

4. Today, Israeli experts M. Zand and M. Altschuler are studying the Bukharan Jews.

MOUNTAIN JEWS

1. J. Cherny, *Book of Travels in the Land of Caucasus and Transcaucasia and Other Lands of Southern Russia* (St Petersburg 1884). (In Hebrew)

2. I.S. Anisimov (ed.), *Caucasian Mountain Jews*, Dashkov Museum of Ethnography Vol. III (Moscow 1888) p. 171-322. (In Russian)

3. M. Bezhanov, *Jews of Vartashen Village. Symposium on Areas and Tribes of the Caucasus* (Tiflis 1894) p. 110-227. (In Russian)

4. B. Miller, 'Tats, Their Habitat and Dialects (Materials and Problems)', in: *Newsletter of the Society for Exploring and Investigating Azerbaijan* 8/7 (Baku 1929). (In Russian)

5. B. Miller, *Kuba Version of the Tat Dialect of Mountain Jews. Materials of IVAN* (1932). (In Russian)

6. M. Agarunov, *Great Destiny of a Small Nation* (Moscow 1995). (In Russian)

7. Today, Israeli scholars M. Zand and M. Altschuler are studying the Mountain Jews.

GEORGIAN JEWS

1. J. Cherny, *Book of Travels in the Land of Caucasus and Transcaucasia and Other Lands of Southern Russia* (St Petersburg 1884). (In Hebrew)

2. R. Arbel and L. Magal (eds), *In the Land of the Golden Fleece. The Jews of Georgia - History and Culture* (Tel Aviv 1992). (In Hebrew and English)

Samarkand Jewish Museum, c. 1930. (Indigenous Jewish Museum Collection, Municipal Museum, Samarkand)

Rabbi with typical Caucasian fur hat, Georgia, late 19th century. Photo by D.I. Ermakov. (Janashia Museum, Georgia)

1167. Еврей. Имер. равин

History and Ethnography Expeditions of St Petersburg Jewish University

In the early twentieth century, St Petersburg was one of the world's foremost centres of Jewish studies, especially history, ethnography and folk studies. Russian Jewish studies came to a halt in the late 1920s and only revived with the advent of *Perestroika* in the USSR. This revival was stimulated by a growing interest in their past among Jewish students, which had begun in Soviet times. In 1988, this interest resulted in a series of field trips by young amateur history students to areas that had once had large Jewish populations and had been involved in major events in Jewish history, primarily the Ukraine and Byelorussia. At first, these expeditions were organised by Ilya Dvorkin, Veniamin Lukin and various enthusiasts from St Petersburg (then still Leningrad).

In 1989, the efforts of this same group led to the foundation of St Petersburg Jewish University, mainly to train participants for new expeditions and to develop field studies; Ilya Dvorkin was appointed rector. Since then regular field trips have been undertaken on an increasingly professional basis and covering ever larger areas. From the start, the expeditions were complex, involving material culture, history, folklore and historical lore. During the past nine years, several hundred people have taken part in expeditions: students and professors of St Petersburg Jewish University, as well as volunteers. Hundreds of towns and shtetls within the former Pale of Settlement, from the Baltic to the Black Sea have been visited. The Institute of Jewish Diaspora Studies was founded as part of the St Petersburg Jewish University to increase the efficiency of the field and academic work; the many objects recovered on the various field trips being stored in the Archives of the University.

In 1992, the Institute began working closely with the Center for Jewish Art at the Hebrew University in Jerusalem, and as a result, the art research program on ritual objects and the study of synagogue architecture in the Jewish communities has become a major part of the Institute's work. The range of studies has also been gradually widened: in 1992, research began into the history of non-Ashkenazi communities of the former USSR, starting with Bukharan Jews and later including the Mountain Jews and Georgian Jews. Expeditions allowed an enormous amount of new material to be registered, saved from oblivion and exposed to the academic world for students of the history and culture of the Jews of the former USSR. Apart from their scientific impact, the expeditions of the St Petersburg Jewish University have always been of special significance to the participants, providing an opportunity to become involved in the history of the Jewish people.

Documenting rimmonim at a Derbent synagogue during a joint expedition of the St Petersburg Jewish University and the Center for Jewish Art, Jerusalem, 1994.

Jewish school, Bukhara, 1890s.
(Russian Museum of Ethnography)

Central Asian Jewish Costume

Tatjana Emelyanenko
Russian Museum of Ethnography, St Petersburg

Traditionally, Russian ethnographic scholars and collectors have placed little emphasis on the Central Asian, or Bukharan Jewish culture, a material and spiritual heritage that has never been studied in any great detail. This appears to have resulted not so much from official race-related policies influencing the development of ethnographic studies and museum policy in pre-revolutionary and Soviet times, but rather from the existence of two different, equally erroneous outlooks on the development of the traditional culture of Oriental Jews common among ethnologists in the nineteenth and twentieth centuries. Jewish culture was considered generally homogeneous and the Jews of the Orient were thought to be little different from the Jews of Europe.
S. Weisenberg, a Russian expert on Central Asian Jews, commented in the early twentieth century on this common misunderstanding that 'it is unfortunately undeniable that anthropologists and ethnographers travelling in non-European countries show little interest in local Jews. This is clearly a manifestation of a deeply rooted view that Jews are a homogeneous people: all Jews are the same as at home. This is a misconception shared by many and is extremely harmful both for the anthropological and ethnographic study of the Jews, since it leads scholars to overlook the Jewish groups even when differences with European Jews are obvious'.[1]

The second perspective implied that the traditional culture of Oriental Jews had lost its authenticity with the extensive contacts with Moslem cultures. This misconception had a certain basis in fact. The peoples of Central Asia and local Jews had shared long centuries of history. According to legend, migrations of descendants of the Babylonian Jews from Iran and Afghanistan began in the first century CE. In the early Middle Ages Jews settled in numerous towns and villages, from Merv, Balkh, Bukhara, Samarkand to the Seven Rivers and Kashgar. Historians and geographers from the ninth to the sixteenth centuries - Narshakhi, Tabari, Biruni, Nisami and Arusi Samarkandi - mention Central Asian Jews and Jewish communities in their chronicles. Jews played an important part in trade on the great Silk Road.[2]

The earliest and strongest Jewish communities were those of Bukhara, Samarkand and Shakhrisabz. Later, Jews settled in other cities, such as Tashkent, Kokand and Andizhan. In fact, the Jewish quarter in Margilan dates from the early nineteenth century, and Jews only settled in Fergana in the early twentieth century. Jews came to the Gissara Valley (Tajikistan) in the mid-nineteenth century, and shortly after established a quarter in Dushanbe. In recent centuries Jewish communities were founded not only in major cities, but in small suburban settlements too.

In the nineteenth century most Jews were living among the Tajiks (the dominant population of Bukhara, Samarkand and Shakhrisabz) as they always had, for the latter were descendants of the native Iranian-speaking peoples of Central Asia, the first to be encountered by Jews. Other local Turkic peoples did not emerge until the sixteenth century and later. In the towns of the Fergana Valley and in Tashkent Jews lived among Uzbeks (or Sartes) - a people of Turkic and Iranian origin - although their culture and lifestyle resembled that of the Tajiks. Jewish communities were also found in the Turkmenian cities of Merv, Iolotan and others. Several Jewish families lived among the Kazakhs. In each case the material culture and lifestyle of each Jewish group came to reflect local Moslem customs. It has not been easy, therefore, for scholars and collectors to identify household objects, traditional clothes or instruments specific to the culture of Central Asian Jews. This is why the ethnographic collections of Central Asia[3] and Russia have never received Jewish items on a regular basis.

Today, the St Petersburg Russian Museum of Ethnography is the only institute in Russia with an ethnographic collection of Central Asian or Bukharan Jewish objects. This modest collection was formed over a period of 150 years. Analysis of the various objects, field research and comparative studies of similar objects and phenomena in local Moslem cultures have enabled scholars to identify and describe particular aspects of the traditional culture of the Central Asian Jews. Scholars discovered that, despite 'many centuries of existence in a

Fortress Gate (Emir's old palace), Bukhara. Photo by S.M. Dudin, 1902.
(Russian Museum of Ethnography)

Moslem Asiatic environment, and the adoption of outward traditions and mores of the surrounding peoples, Jews continued to remain a distinct group.'[4]

The earliest Bukharan Jewish items purchased date from the late 1860s and early 1870s. These are a man's costume and a separate hat. They belong to the so-called Turkestan or Kaufman collection of over 3,000 pieces displayed in 1872 together with other ethnographic objects relating to the peoples of the Russian Empire at the All Russian Polytechnic Exhibition in Moscow. The Exhibition was inspired and arranged by the Imperial Society for Natural History, Anthropology and Ethnography, to celebrate the bicentenary of Peter the Great.[5] In 1902 numerous exhibits were given to the Dashkov Museum of Ethnography (Moscow),[6] renamed the Museum of Ethnic Studies in 1924 (later the Museum of the Peoples of the USSR); in 1948 the museum closed, and the ethnographic collections, including the Bukharan Jewish collection, were transferred to St Petersburg.[7]

Numerous Russian scholars, members of the Society for Natural History, Anthropology and Ethnography, helped prepare the 1872 exhibition. One, a young natural history student named Alexey Fedchenko, was engaged in research in Turkestan.[8] The governor general of Turkestan, K.P. von Kaufman,[9] provided substantial logistical and financial support. Local ethnographers and intellectuals were also involved in the research. Unfortunately, the identity of most collectors and information about where most of the items were purchased was not recorded. This applies, for example, to the Bukharan Jewish costume, described briefly in the exhibition catalogue as 'mannequin of a Turkestan Jew'.[10] Nonetheless, indirect evidence may provide a more precise attribution.

The costume is of a common Central Asian type, consisting of two gowns - one light, with no lining (cat. no. 20) worn over or instead of a shirt, and one outer wadded gown (cat. no. 21), headgear, including a hat (cat. no. 23) and a skull cap (cat. no. 24), a long wide scarf used as a belt (cat. no. 22) and a pair of boots (cat. no. 25). Just as the cut, the trimmings, the fabric and the style of a person's garments identified their ethnic or local origins, the clothes worn by Jews differed from one area to the other, with local variations often reflecting the general traditions of the region. Analysis of the costume displayed at the 1872 exhibition shows that it belonged to a Jew from Samarkand. This is revealed principally by the cut of the gowns, which is typical of this city,[11] as well as the handmade materials, the cotton *kalami* (the light gown) and silk *shoyi* (the outer gown). Both, judging by the technology and colours, were produced in Samarkand. In addition, the skull cap is characteristic of Samarkand. Small cloth caps were popular in Central Asia, where they were worn underneath a felt or fur hat, under a turban or separately, at home and in public. Originally, the shape, material and embroidery would have reflected the owner's ethnic and regional background. The striped silk upper gown, scarf-belt and ornate velvet hat with fur trimmings are particularly noteworthy: this combination was rare at that time, unique to Jews living under the Turkestan governorship of 1867 - the area conquered by Russia in Kazakhstan and Kokand - to which Samarkand was added in 1868.[12]

Jewish man and child, Samarkand, 1902.
Photo by S.M. Dudin.
(Russian Museum of Ethnography)

Selling silk thread at the bazar, Samarkand, 1933. (Indigenous Jewish Museum Collection, Municipal Museum, Samarkand)

Group of Bukharan Jews. Photo by D.I. Ermakov, 1890–1910s. (Russian Museum of Ethnography)

Before the Russian conquest, Central Asian Jews had endured a series of 21 prohibitions known as the Omar Conditions.[13] These had been introduced to divide Jews from the Moslem population, to limit their freedom of movement and to encourage them to convert to Islam. The restrictions affected trade, public conduct, property rights and the clothes that could be worn, specifically gowns, belts and hats. Wolf, one of the first Europeans to visit Bukhara, wrote in 1832, that 'Jews were not allowed to trim their gowns with silk'[14] (i.e. with silk ribbon or fringes – T.E.). Other scholars mentioned that 'Jews are not allowed to wear gowns of bright or multiple colours […] just the black or brown *alacha* gowns'[15] (i.e. made of handmade cotton cloth). Jews 'could not come to the market'[16] without dark undecorated outer gowns.

Belts formed an integral part of a man's clothing in Central Asia. Some were made of leather, some of a square cloth, diagonally folded, or of scarves of various fabrics. Bukharan Jews were forced to wear a rough horsehair rope, placed just below the chest, 'and so that they would not conceal this so-called 'sign of distinction', they were strictly forbidden to wear a non-belted gown over a belted one'.[17] While some Jews managed to buy permission to replace the rope with a leather belt,[18] cloth belts remained the prerogative of Moslems.

Restrictions on headgear were particularly severe. It was a capital offence for a Jew to wear a turban. Jews had to wear 'a square cap of lustrine or glued calico, always black and trimmed with lambskin'.[19] A cap of this type was acquired for the St Petersburg collection in 1926, revealing the persistence of the custom.

With the establishment of the Turkestan governorship, Jews acquired equal rights with Moslems, and all the humiliating prohibitions and restrictions were lifted, including the dress restrictions. These survived only in the Bukharan Emirate, which remained an independent state under Russian protection. While the gown, belt and hat of the costume discussed here must have been worn by a Jew from Russian Turkestan; the details of the gowns and skull cap place the costume in Samarkand.

Another Jewish hat (cat. no. 26) was shown separately at the Polytechnic exhibition of 1872, in the section devoted to headdresses of various peoples. It is made of a less expensive material than the one belonging to the costume, representing an everyday, ordinary type of hat worn in Samarkand, Tashkent and other Turkestan cities.

Although this costume is the only example in the collection, it reveals some of the details of the clothes worn by Jewish men and reflects the changes that took place under the Turkestan governorship, particularly in Samarkand. It is interesting to see how quickly these took hold. The costume dates from before 1869, the year Fedchenko spent several months in Samarkand, the city with the largest Jewish community in the region. Here he resided in the large Jewish quarter, *Mahalla-i-Yahudin* (established in 1843). His objective was to collect material for the exhibition (by 1870 the entire Turkestan collection was compiled and ready). Samarkand was not incorporated into the Turkestan governorship until 1868. Moslem dress did not change in that short period. On the other hand, as soon as they could, Jews abandoned the humiliating sign of distinction. Contemporary photographs and analysis of museum objects reveal that the 'ethnic' and 'local' conservatism of dress and other everyday devices typical of Islamic dress, especially among local Moslems, was not reflected in the conduct of the Central Asian Jews. They kept their religious customs and protected their traditions, but in everyday life they were much more open to new cultural influences and often encouraged the introduction of the latter in the Moslem world. Jews were therefore willing to break the local pattern of their dress and introduce non-local details, changing the cut and colour.

Jewish boy, Samarkand.
Photo by S.M. Dudin, 1902.
(Russian Museum of Ethnography)

Jewish girl, Samarkand.
Photo by S.M. Dudin, 1902.
(Russian Museum of Ethnography)

Naturally, this, more than particular elements of the costume, determined its specific character, at least in the later decades of the nineteenth century in Turkestan, and it distinguished the costume worn by Jews from that of their Moslem neighbours.

After the exhibition of 1872, no items relating to Central Asian Jewish ethnography were acquired until 1926. In that year, S.P. Preobragensky,[20] curator of the Museum of Ethnic Studies in Moscow, undertook a field trip to Bukhara, Samarkand and Ura-Tyube. The main aim was to collect items relating to Tajik ethnography, yet in Samarkand he also purchased a small collection of local Jewish items (cat. nos 1-19). He deliberately chose objects that revealed a contrast between Jewish and Moslem cultures. The Preobragensky collection therefore consisted mainly of religious items, with just three exceptions: a woman's gown, a man's hat and a skull cap - carefully selected as examples of ethnic distinctiveness.

At first glance, the gown (cat. no. 3), called a *munisak* in Samarkand and a *kaltacha* in Bukhara and Nurata, does not appear to differ from those worn by Tajik and Uzbek women. Derived from an ancient type of garment, in the second half of the nineteenth century it was used as ritual attire, gradually disappearing in the early twentieth century.[21] Jews wore the *munisak* only during mourning: women of the deceased person's family would wear it indoors for the first seven days of mourning, when they were not allowed outside.[22] Gowns of this type were made of various fabrics of different colours, depending on the age and wealth of the owner. Bukharan Jews used similar types of fabrics, although they preferred silk or semi-silk homespun cloth with narrow blue or green stripes - this fabric was known in Central Asia as a typically Jewish fabric, although it was produced by the Tajiks and the Uzbeks. It is hard to find a reason for this, but it is encountered repeatedly in the studies of traditional weaving and fabrics of Central Asia as one of the distinctive features of Jewish dress.[23]

Another distinctive ethnic feature of the gown is in the history and spread of its use. According to Preobragensky, it was purchased in Samarkand but manufactured in Bukhara,[24] which is confirmed by its distinctive cut, trimmings, cloth type and other details typical of the Bukharan *kaltacha*.[25] The Moslems of Central Asia were still remarkably conservative about their ritual clothes, including the *munisak*. Even in the twentieth century these clothes retained distinctive local features (e.g. the cut and the fabric), often related to ancient religious concepts. For Jews, on the other hand, it was sufficient that ritual attire complied with general standards, without the specific local details.

Of the two items of headgear in the Preobragensky collection, the hat with a black *Astrakhan* band (cat. no. 1) is especially typical: Central Asian Jews were supposed to wear these hats under the Omar Conditions. The skull cap (cat. no. 2) was one of several Central Asian soft cloth cap varieties worn underneath fur hats; it also had certain distinctive features. These caps were not normally made of light coloured fabrics or festooned with fringes (except those made for children). These were not typical for Samarkand, where this example was obtained, or other cities of the area, where a turban was the common form of headgear among Moslems, with a different cap generally worn underneath (skull cap cat. no. 24). Perhaps Jews wore these skull caps for worship and religious rites, and perhaps this was why it was purchased by Preobragensky, who was primarily concerned with religious items.

The latter included various amulets with prayers and spells, *tefillin* with cases and a *tallit katan* – this apparently being the extent of religious objects owned by the Central Asian Jews. European Ashkenazim, visiting Central Asia, were always amazed at the plainness and relative austerity of the religious items used by Bukharan Jews. Thus, Weisenberg commented that local synagogues have few utensils, 'no stylish candelabra, no candlesticks, no Hanukkah lamps, no kiddush cups [...] Most locals could not even understand my questions about these items. They sit on the floor, and the only ornamentation, apart from the carpets and the draperies, are the amulets with pictures of Jerusalem, framed and displayed on the walls [...] the houses of Central Asian Jews look equally bare. No Sabbath lamp, no Seder plate, no *hadas* for Havdalah [...]'.[26] The few religious items for synagogue or home use that Bukharan Jews possessed, were mostly imported from Jerusalem and, after connections had been established in the late eighteenth century,[27] from Eastern European Jewish communities.

Most of the religious items in the Preobragensky collection were imported. Yet their use, decoration and the names reflect specific local religious and cultural traditions. Thus, the *tallit katan* (cat. no. 4), classically shaped and made of white cloth with *zizit* tassels, was, according to the collector, referred to as a *beged* (garment) and tablets with the names for God were sewn into its fringes,[28] which was actually counter to religious custom. To judge from the knots on the straps and the script, the head and hand *tefillin* (cat. no. 5) and the cases (cat. no. 6) are of Sephardi type, corresponding to the Sephardi ritual of the Bukharan Jews. They were brought to Central Asia from Palestine. Most of the bags in which they were kept were handmade. Homespun and factory-made cloth, embroidery and elaborately patterned ribbon were used for one of the bags

Jewish school in Samarkand.
Photo by S.M. Dudin, 1902.
(Russian Museum of Ethnography)

(cat. no. 8). The other bag in the Preobragensky collection (cat. no. 7) was manufactured in Russia, probably commissioned by a local merchant who travelled there on business. This bag was made of machine-made velveteen, decorated with gold embroidery, a heraldic and foliate design as well as inscriptions: the name of the owner in Hebrew - Moshe, son of the late Avraham Binyamin - and the date - 1893. Judging by the quality of the gold thread, it was manufactured at the Moscow factory of Konstantin Alexeyev (known as Stanislavsky), and the embroidery technique is typical for Torzhok, a well-known Russian centre of gold embroidery.

Amulets with religious quotations or spells, worn as charms on the body or displayed on the wall, were popular among the entire Jewish population. Here there is a definite similarity between Bukharan Jews and local Moslems, for whom amulets with Qur'an quotations (or simply Arabic letters) were the only comparable religious items. Of nine amulets in the Preobragensky collection, one is clearly of local origin (cat. no. 12) since the inscription differs from the usual pattern and is in Judeo-Tajik; the rest, judging by the collector's notes, the paper type and decoration, were brought from Palestine in the 1860s and later. They were made of paper or parchment, with handwritten or printed Hebrew texts. Those include amulets known locally as *chordevoli* (Tajik for 'four walls'), which were placed on the four walls of the room to protect the mother and the baby during labour and delivery (cat. nos 14, 17, 15), a parchment *shivviti* tablet (local *mioro*) with quotations from prayers recited during daily worship (cat. no. 16), a *mezuzah* (local *mzuzo*, cat. no. 9), *komsa* amulets with spells and Cabalistic signs to scare away evil spirits, that were used on a variety of occasions (cat. nos 10, 11, 12, 13).[29]

The same collection contains a High Holidays postcard (cat. no. 18) and a letter from the management of Misgav-Ladach maternity hospital in Jerusalem asking for donations (cat. no. 19) - which testifies to the links between Bukharan Jews and the Holy Land. In exchange for Hebrew books,[30] Bukharan Jews made occasional contributions to charities in Jerusalem.[31]

The Preobragensky collection provided new ethnographic data on the dress of Central Asian Jews and added items relating to religion and ritual. Yet the acquisitions of 1869 and 1926 were a meagre reflection of the world of Bukharan Jewish material culture. Nevertheless, despite their limited number and diversity, these items served as a foundation for further studies of the culture of this ethnic group at the St Petersburg museum, where they were transferred in 1948. There was no special emphasis on the Bukharan Jews in the museum's collection policy. Items were apparently acquired at random. For example, the large collections of early Central Asian objects (over 2,000 items), contributed by the distinguished ethnographer, artist and photographer Samuel Dudin[32] in 1900-1902, contain few pieces of Jewish interest.

Women's *kulutapushak* caps, Bukhara and Samarkand (cat. nos 31, 32, 30, 52)

Costume listed as 'Mannequin of a Turkestan Jew' in the All Russian Polytechnic Exhibition in Moscow in 1872 (cat. nos 20-25)

Munisak, woman's ritual garment worn during mourning, Samarkand (cat. no. 3)

42

Costumes of a Bukharan man and woman
(cat. nos 37, 45, 50, 55, 62)

Poncha, bracelets, Samarkand
(cat. no. 27)

Bracelets, Bukhara
(cat. nos 35, 36)

Nosi gardan, breast ornament, Bukhara
(cat. no 63)

45

Woman's costume, Tashkent (cat. nos 47, 49, 57, 61)
Woman's costume, Samarkand (cat. no. 46)
Paranja, Bukhara (cat. no. 51)

Bukharan dress
with *peshkurta* band
(cat. no. 44)

Rimmonim, Tashkent
(cat. no. 76)

Tefillin with cases and bag,
Samarkand
(cat. nos 5-7)

One characteristic item is a *tallit* purchased in Samarkand (cat. no. 34). It is a strip of light handmade serge silk, with dark stripes at the ends, and to judge from the cloth, it was manufactured by Samarkand weavers[33] who often worked for the Jewish community. Another obviously Jewish piece is a gilt drinking glass with chiselled pattern and blue pasta inlay (cat. no. 125), shaped like the traditional Sabbath kiddush cup. Although it was probably made by a Tajik jeweller in Bukhara as a *piola* (a traditional teacup), a vessel of this shape, and one intended for drinking wine, would never have been used by a Moslem, and must therefore be identified as belonging to the Jewish culture.

As for the other pieces, Dudin's notes indicate that they were used both by local Moslems and Jews – for example the women's *kulutapushak* caps, various items of jewellery and fabrics. A *kulutapushak* is a cap with a pouch attached to hold the hair; they were widely worn throughout Central Asia. Yet Dudin noted that by the beginning of the twentieth century the local women in major cities like Bukhara or Samarkand regarded them as obsolete and provincial, and had stopped wearing them; they were only worn by Jewish women.[34] Most local *kulutapushaks* were made of simple cotton cloth trimmed with a coloured band, while the caps worn by Jewish women were made of opulent, expensive cloth, richly embroidered. Jewish women of Samarkand, Shakhrisabz and adjacent areas wore *kulutapushaks* with multicoloured silk embroidery in iroqui (half-cross) stitch with stylized foliate patterns (cat. nos 29, 30, 31, 32). They were made in Shakhrisabz, where the Tajik embroiderers specialized in this technique and where workshops had been founded in the second half of the nineteenth century supplying embroidered horse blankets, men's gowns, curtains etc. to the court of the Bukharan Emir. Jewish women from Bukhara used to wear *kulutapushaks* with gold embroidery (cat. no. 33) – a style unique to this city.

Ornate *kulutapushaks* were expensive. Yet their opulence seems strangely misplaced considering the complexity of Jewish women's headgear and the *kulutapushak*'s place underneath, covered by various scarves, and almost never seen. Obviously, the rich ornamentation and the fact that they remained part of Jewish costume for so long, suggests some special significance relating to traditional symbols or the now obscure history of the introduction of *kulutapushaks* to Jewish dress. Whatever the reason, this archaic headgear remained in vogue until the first decades of the twentieth century, while other elements of Jewish dress were changing drastically.

Of the handmade fabrics in Dudin's collection, one was produced by Jewish craftsmen – a batik material known in Tajik as *gulbast*. This was used for shawls (cat. nos 123, 81) and women's dresses (cat. no. 80, 82) and was common in both Jewish and Moslem costume. Weaving was not a Jewish trade, but Jews were prominent in the dyeing industry, especially indigo. This was a respectable trade, and was traditionally believed to have been practised by their Jewish ancestors in Iran. Jewish dye workshops were located in Samarkand, Bukhara, Margilan, Karmana and Merv.[35] Many of the multicoloured or striped fabrics, *ikat*, produced by Tajik or Uzbek weavers in those cities would therefore have

been in part the product of Jewish craftsmanship. Moreover, the best batik designs were traditionally produced by Jewish craftsmen.

Among the many pieces of jewellery in the Dudin collection, two have been identified as having been worn by local Jewish women: a necklace, manufactured in Bukhara of gilded mastic plates with pearls and coloured stones (cat. no. 28) and twin bracelets of stringed silver pendants and coral, made in Samarkand (cat. no. 27). Similar pieces manufactured by Tajik jewellers were worn by local Tajik women, which makes it difficult to distinguish ethnic features in the shape or decoration, especially since traditional ethnic and local features had already started to die out earlier in Central Asian jewellery, and in Bukhara and Samarkand in the second half of the nineteenth century.[36] Jewish jewellery differed not so much in shape, as in material, in the more extensive use of gold, whereas Moslems traditionally preferred silver which they endowed with special magic powers. Gold ornaments had not been produced until the late nineteenth century, and then mostly in Bukhara, when trade connections with Central Asia had developed and gold, brought in bars from Russia, had become more easily available. They were made in the workshops of Tajiks and Bukharan Jews to the same pattern as traditional local silver ornaments and were worn together with the latter on wedding or festive dresses. Yet among Moslems it was only the rulers, their wives and associates who would have worn gold jewellery as a status symbol.[37] Besides ornaments, Jewish jewellers made gilt dishes, gilt-silver and gold objects and traditional Moslem items, but in pure gold. Gold bracelets were particularly popular. Twin bracelets of this type were acquired by the St Petersburg museum in 1988 (cat. nos 35, 36). This was the first contribution to the Central Asian Jewish collection after a gap of almost 60 years. They were contributed by a private donor, T.G. Ginzburg, whose family had lived in Bukhara in the late nineteenth century. Silver bracelets of a similar shape (a flexible plaque with a hinge-type lock, the shift of which was called a 'key', and open-carving) were manufactured by Tajik and Uzbek craftsmen in Samarkand and Tashkent, although the best examples came from Bukhara. It was in Bukhara, among the Jewish jewellers, that they were first manufactured in gold.

In Bukhara in the same year the author purchased a woman's shawl (cat. no. 37), dating from the late nineteenth century.[38] Triangular in shape and made of tulle-type fabric, it resembles the shawls brought to Central Asia from adjacent Oriental countries which remained in common use until the early twentieth century. It is decorated on top with metal spangles (*pulyak* in Tajik) in foliate designs, floral rosettes and similar motifs. According to the local Jews, these were only worn by Jews. Others, such as Uzbeks and Tajiks, wore similar shawls but not embroidered. They were worn over the *kulutapushak* cap, or another shawl, or a band, with the ends crossed under the chin and tied at the back. Archive photos show that this way of wearing shawls was exclusive to Central Asian Jews. Moslem women left the ends hanging loose in front or at the back, or both.

In 1994 a wooden Torah scroll case (cat. no. 40) was donated to the museum by St Petersburg Jewish University, which had been purchased on a field

Jewish women and children, Samarkand. Photo by S.M. Dudin, 1902. (Russian Museum of Ethnography)

Family of a rich Jew in front of a sukkah, Samarkand. Photo by S.M. Dudin, 1902. (Russian Museum of Ethnography)

Chordevoli, amulet to protect mother and child, hung on the four walls of the delivery room, late 19th century. (cat. no. 17).

expedition at the synagogue in Kokand. In Central Asian synagogues Torah scrolls were often the only religious items. They were kept in a niche in the western wall and the ornamentation differed considerably from the Ashkenazi style. Weisenberg, who studied local synagogues in the early twentieth century, wrote that 'instead of our cloth covers, they keep the scrolls in wooden boxes, usually veneered with silver. Instead of a crown, the rollers (*atsei hayyim*) are decorated with *rimmonim*, which adorn the *bimah* corners during the service. Both the pointers (*yad*) and the boards are of plain design'.[39] Torah scrolls were the most valuable items in the synagogue, from a spiritual and material point of view. They came to Central Asia from Europe or Palestine, like the other religious artifacts.

The Torah case was also imported. Although the collectors discovered it among pieces that had been abandoned and could not determine either when it had last been used or its background, there is some indirect evidence to suggest its origin. The wood processing technique and the structure are not typical of Central Asian craftsmanship, and the upholstery is definitely European. This fabric, known as patterned velvet (a velvet ornament on the plain background, with thin metal thread, introduced into the base alongside silk thread) was manufactured in Lyon (France) and Venice (Italy). It was the most expensive material of its kind and was used as upholstery in palaces and wealthy homes. By the end of the nineteenth century the complex technique involved had been almost completely abandoned. Thus, judging from the material, the Kokand Torah scroll case appears to have been made no later than the second half of the nineteenth century and was probably brought to Central Asia around the same period.

In 1994 two women's dresses from the Fergana Valley town of Margilan, 20 kilometres from Fergana and at one time the site of a large Jewish quarter, were sent to the museum. Judging by the cut and type of fabric, both dresses date from the first decades of the twentieth century. One (cat. no. 38) is made of machine-made jaccardy silk which was produced by Russian factories and exported to Central Asia between 1880 and 1920. The second (cat. no. 39) is made of striped silk satin, produced in small local workshops in the 1920s or 1930s. Both dresses resemble the style of tunic, with no shoulder seams and a straight torso (the cloth was not cut with scissors, but torn) that had been widespread in Central Asia. In the 1920s, these tunics had virtually disappeared, particularly in the cities. They were substituted by more elaborate cuts - with shoulder seams, a cut-in sleeve and a yoke, and these still remain the most popular type in the area.

The cut is not only a guide to the date of manufacture, it also helps visualize how the Jews of the Fergana Valley dressed in the late nineteenth and early twentieth centuries. In general, the garment resembles those worn by the local Tajik and Uzbek women: long rather loose (bodice and skirt are almost of the same width), with long straight sleeves and stand-up collar, together with a vertical cut at the collar, concealed by a flap with buttons or studs. Stand-up collars (*nogai yoka*, i.e. 'Tartar collar') replaced the horizontal or vertical cut with

Jewish woman wearing a shawl decorated with spangles, Samarkand. Photo by S.M. Dudin, 1902.

Silk dyeing workshop, Samarkand. Photo by S.M. Dudin, 1902.

Synagogue, Bukhara, 1890s. (Russian Museum of Ethnography)

laces typical of Central Asia generally, and became popular in the cities of the Fergana Valley (Fergana, Kokand and Margilan) as well as Tashkent in the 1880s and 1890s. At first the Moslems distrusted the new fashion, condemning it as sinful. The stand-up collar was initially adopted by merchants and entrepreneurs, the kind of circles to which many Jews belonged. Jewish dresses normally had a wider bodice and sleeves than those worn by the Moslem women of Fergana Valley, who were starting to make their dresses increasingly tight. The former are closer to the traditional Bukharan dresses, known in the area for their loose cut.

A remarkable aspect is that both dresses have been preserved for over sixty years, indeed one has never actually been worn. This meticulous care, even for clothes which were not used, is typical of Central Asia. According to a local tradition that still survives, an abundance of clothes and other household items is a sign of wealth and prosperity and of good fortune. Particular items would have been reminders of important events. Moreover, throwing a garment away was a sin, since it was a product of human labour. Dowries would comprise a wealth of material and clothes, sometimes more than could be used in an entire lifetime. But meanwhile, economic development, expansion of trade and new cultural influences were causing the traditional lifestyle to disappear and bringing changes in the traditional designs of clothes. Many dresses of a more traditional cut which women had received at their wedding in the late nineteenth and early twentieth centuries were never used. These were carefully preserved by the families and passed to subsequent generations. This has proved an invaluable source for modern researchers of local costume, including students of Jewish dress.

Jewish girl wearing an amulet, Samarkand.
Photo by S.M. Dudin, 1902.
(Russian Museum of Ethnography)

Clearly then, in Russian ethnography little consistency has been shown in the collection of Jewish ethnographic material from Central Asia. Instead of formulating policies, collection was left to the enthusiasm of certain ethnographers whose intuition ensured that this remarkable cultural phenomenon was not neglected. It was only in 1995, with the prospect of the present exhibition, that the St Petersburg collection was examined and a decision was taken, despite the time already lost, to expand the Jewish collection and to improve the presentation of the traditions and customs of this ethnic group.

With the disintegration of the USSR and the formation of independent states in Central Asia a new and considerable obstacle has arisen. A Tashkent collector called Viktor Viktorovich Kucherov, who has been in contact with the St Petersburg museum for a number of years was commissioned to acquire pieces for the collection. This he has been doing for the past two years and presently there are more than fifty pieces: dresses, jewellery, household utensils and a set of *rimmonim*. Each is described in detail - time and place of manufacture and use, names of owners and so forth. Most pieces date from the late nineteenth to early twentieth centuries.

The bulk of the collection comprises women's dresses, gowns, shawls, caps, forehead bands (33 pieces), i.e. those items that would have been preserved the

Woman wearing a *paranja* and a *chachvan*, Samarkand, early 20th century.
(Indigenous Jewish Museum Collection, Municipal Museum, Samarkand)

The ketubah, marriage contract, completed during the wedding ceremony by the man seated in front, late 19th – early 20th century.
(Private collection V.V. Kucherov, Tashkent)

Family of Bukharan Jews, the girl is holding a *chachvan* in her hand, Bukhara, 1890s.
(Russian Museum of Ethnography)

longest by local people. These were purchased by Kucherov in Bukhara, Tashkent and Kokand, and provide a comprehensive picture of what Jewish women wore in this area. It is clear that these items of clothing are largely similar to those worn by the Tajik and Uzbek women of the area. The Bukharan dresses, for example, (cat. nos 41-46) are characterized by loose waistlines and sleeves, according to the Bukharan fashions of the turn of the century; Bukharan women normally wore two or three dresses over each other (the top one being the most exquisite, the ones featured in this collection) to give the impression of a sturdy build, which was a sign of prosperity and therefore the standard of beauty of the day. Tashkent (cat. no. 47) and Kokand (cat. no. 48) dresses, which were close in style in the late nineteenth century, reveal a slimmer cut, with a stand-up collar and a flap with buttons or studs, as in the Margilan dresses described above (cat. nos 38, 39). In Bukhara it was customarily to fix a long, almost full-length, exquisitely embroidered strap (*peshkurta*) to the collar of the upper dress. In the Kucherov collection the *peshkurta* is decorated with Shakhrisabz needlework (like the *kulutapushak* caps, cat. nos 29, 30 etc.) or gold embroidery; Bukharan Tajiks used similar bands for their dresses. The fabrics are handmade - striped semi-silk *bekasab*, silk *ikat shoyi* and semi-silk *ikat adras*. As already noted, the choice of fabric is exclusive to Jewish dresses. Thus, two are made of striped silk manufactured by the Tajiks of Karatag village in Gissara Valley, known as *alochaï karatagi* (cat. no. 46) and *bekasab* from Kitab, a town not far from Shakhrisabz (cat. no. 45). With their extensive trade connections, Bukharan markets were well supplied with high quality fabrics, but the local Moslems used them exclusively for men's gowns, predominantly for the wardrobes of noblemen. *Adras* from Bukhara and Gizhduvan workmanship (Gizhduvan is a town 70 kilometres from Bukhara) were used exclusively for men's gowns, yet, Jewish dresses for women were made of the same material. Today, these details may seem insignificant to those unfamiliar with the history of the manufacture and use of handmade fabrics in Central Asia, but at the turn of the century the material of a dress was important, presenting a significant and meticulously observed sign of ethnicity, social status, sex and age.

Women's gowns in the Kucherov collection (cat. nos 49, 50) and the only men's garment (cat. no. 62) belong to the type of tailored garments introduced into Central Asia in the late nineteenth century to replace the traditional tunic. Tailored clothes, especially gowns with cut-in sleeves, shoulder seams and waistline spread under the influence of another Central Asian Moslem people, the Tartars. Even so, the local population was rather slow in adopting this new style. It was first taken up in circles of intellectuals, governmental officials, merchants in Tashkent and the Fergana Valley towns, who absorbed the new Russian influences, and only in the 1920s and 1930s did it spread to other areas. Nevertheless, most archive photos of the late nineteenth and early twentieth centuries show both Jewish men and women wearing garments of this cut. It reveals that they were among the first in the area to adopt the new fashion - even in the highly conservative city of Bukhara (where tailored clothes were only

Jewish women, c. 1890. (Russian Museum of Ethnography)

Mazzah rolling pin, Tashkent
(cat. no. 75)

Wine vessel and household
artifacts, Tashkent
(cat. nos 74, 66-71)

Making mazzot for Passover, 1935.
(Indigenous Jewish Museum Collection, Municipal Museum, Samarkand)

generally accepted in the 1930s). The gowns in the Kucherov collection are from Bukhara and date from no later than the 1890s.

Women's headgear is represented in the collection by a *kulutapushak* cap (cat. no. 52), similar to the one described above (cat. no. 33), and a small round cap, covered in gold embroidery (cat. no. 53). The latter was worn exclusively by Central Asian Jews, although similar caps were worn by young girls in the Tajik communities of Samarkand, Bukhara and mountain villages; yet, in the late nineteenth century they were considered out of fashion.[40] Even so, in all the Jewish communities of the area the tradition was preserved as a hat for young girls and young married women; these caps were also characterized by rich gold embroidery and were worn in specific style with the upper part bent and twisted to one side, like a pilot's cap.

The forehead bands and shawls acquired by Kucherov were once part of a complex headdress worn by married women, similar to that worn by local Moslems. Forehead bands (*peshonaband*) might be represented by a folded scarf, a triangular piece of cloth or a special hard cloth band with gold embroidery at the front (cat. nos 54, 55, 56). The latter were worn by young women. *Peshonabands* were worn over a shawl or a *kulutapushak* cap, with another shawl over this. In the 1890s, the shawls worn in Central Asia were made in factories in Russia; there are a number in the collection (cat. no. 57) which were worn by local women, including Jewish women, at the turn of the century.

The last item of clothing in the Kucherov collection is a *paranja* or veil (cat. no. 51). The cut, the fabric and the trimmings are similar to that employed by the settled urban population of Central Asia. It is worth mentioning that

BUKHARAN JEWISH WINE SONG IN HEBREW

This popular party song about wine appears in several manuscript versions from the late sixteenth to the early twentieth centuries, the earliest being engraved on a copper flask in 1583, the most recent being copied in Samarkand in the 1930s. The first letters of each line make the name of the author, Jacob. Translated from Hebrew into Russian by M. Nosonovsky.
(Courtesy of M. Nosonovsky, St Petersburg)

My friend, give me wine quickly
That will shine like an eye.
It will give you more wisdom
For which there is a source.

The heart of the drinker will rejoice.
And then he will reveal the secrets of his heart,
As a Tsar at his meal.
Many are the secrets of wine.

The one who drinks it will forget his poverty
And will not remember the sorrows of his soul.
The commandment: to make Kiddush over it,
Sweet is the Kiddush over wine.

Let's go, brother, into my garden
To make friends and drink wine of my vine.
We shall be singing together.
Many are the songs about wine.

My enemy is with you in the shadows.
Do not drink too much wine,
For too much oil extinguishes the lamp.
The same is true about drinking too much.

The voice of my friend - here he comes -
With much love and much benevolence,
There's no more hard feelings in the heart.
Wine drinking brings peace.

Listen, brother, to the words of my lips,
Let the song of my twittering be pleasant,
It is like honey.
Sweet is the sleep after wine.

On Sabbath night, the commandment is important
To drink wine, as was ordered
by my God, my Strength, the Dwelling of love.
Sacrifice is pouring of wine.

On Sabbath day - Kiddush and Havdalah.
I will bless God the Almighty
I will sing his glory day and night.
He will reveal the treasures of wine.

Central Asian Jewish women suffered fewer restrictions in behaviour and social life than their Moslem neighbours. Thus, they did not have to cover their faces at home and were not supposed to avoid Jewish men. However, in the street, and especially outside the Jewish quarter, they had to wear a *paranja* and cover their face with a horsehair net (*chachvan* or *chashmband*), to comply with the traditions of the Moslem world.

The various pieces of Bukharan jewellery in the Kucherov collection - gold earrings (cat. no. 65), a bracelet (cat. no. 64), a breast ornament, *nosi gardan* (cat. no. 63), provide new insights into the jewellery worn by Central Asian Jews, while they also reveal the similarity to the items worn by Moslems, despite the more extensive use of gold.

Household artifacts from the turn of the century purchased by Kucherov from Jewish families of Tashkent and Bukhara are also similar to typical Moslem items - bowls (cat. nos 66, 67), trays (cat. nos 71, 72, 73), pestle and mortar (cat. no. 70), ladles (cat. no. 68, 69). These were made by Tajik and Uzbek craftsmen, sold at the markets and were available to everyone. Pieces used exclusively by the Jews were a spiked rolling-pin for *mazzah* (cat. no. 75) and a *khum*, a ceramic vessel for storing wine (cat. no. 74). According to the collector, the vessel had been kept in the basement of a Jewish house in Bukhara, and had not been used for many years, since they had switched to buying ritual wine. Nevertheless, it had been treasured as a family heirloom.

The only religious item in the Kucherov collection is a pair of *rimmonim* (cat. no. 76) that once belonged to a Tashkent synagogue. Like the other religious pieces acquired by the museum - and that applies generally to Central Asian religious items - these were not of local origin, having been imported to Central Asia from Europe or Palestine.

The Kucherov items are an important addition to the St Petersburg collection. It has extended and specified the information on the traditional material culture of the Central Asian Jews, which is rapidly becoming harder to describe as the evidence disappears.
In addition to material cultural items, the museum also has a collection of around fifty photographs. These are of great interest not only because of their ethnic value, but because of their history.[41]

The photographs cover a period from the second half of the nineteenth to the early twentieth century. The earliest were taken in the late 1860s and early 1870s. These are several portraits of Jews from Bukhara, Samarkand and Tashkent that were included in albums prepared for the All Russian Polytechnic Exhibition in Moscow (1872) under the title *Ethnic Types from the Turkestan Area*, or *Turkestan Album Ordered by Governor General, General-Adjunct K.P. von Kaufman 1, Compiled by A.L. Kun, 1871-1872* and *Ethnic Types of Central Asia*, both in the museum collection.

A well-known military artist V.V. Vereshagin worked in the Turkestan area in the late 1860s. He was invited by Kaufman to compile an illustrated book on the ethnography of Central Asia. In 1874 the book was ready and published in St Petersburg under the title, *Turkestan. Painted on Location by V.V. Vereshagin,*

Published by the Order of Turkestan Governor General. 26 Pages, 106 Paintings. Among the highly detailed images of the representatives of various ethnic groups, Vereshagin included four portraits of Bukharan Jews (two men and two women). The museum possesses a damaged copy of the first edition and a copy of a later edition, published in Munich.

An extensive selection of photographs by a well-known photographer of the day, Dmitry Ermakov, whose studio specialized in ethnic subjects, date from the 1880s and 1890s. The museum collection includes six photographs featuring groups of Bukharan Jews, local *yeshivot*, Sabbath prayers at the synagogue and Sukkot.

Samarkand Jews are the most widely represented in the museum photo collection. Apart from the portraits already mentioned, the museum possesses 30 photographs taken by Dudin in 1902 in the Jewish quarter of Samarkand. The collection features men, women and children in traditional dress, streets, houses and courtyards of the quarter, classes in the *yeshiva*, synagogue interiors and some of the Sukkot rituals. An excellent photographer and an expert on Central Asia, Dudin chose the most typical ethnic scenes, making his pictures an invaluable source of ethnographic information.

The most recent photo of Bukharan Jews in the St Petersburg collection was taken by F.A. Fielstrup, a museum curator, in the streets of the Bukharan Jewish quarter in 1926 during a field trip. Apart from the dearth of new material, the lack of academic interest in the history of this ethnic group also brought an end to the flow of photos.

דּוֹדִי מַהֵר תְּנָה יַיִן אֲשֶׁר יָאִיר כְּמוֹ עַיִן
וְהוּא יוֹסִיף לְךָ חָכְמָה אֲשֶׁר נִמְצֵאת יֵשׁ מֵאַיִן

יִשְׁתַּחוּ אִישׁ וְיִשְׂמַח לִבּוֹ וְאָז יֹאמַר סוֹדוֹת לִבּוֹ
דּוֹמֶה לַמֶּלֶךְ בְּמִסְבּוֹ רַבִּים הָמָה סוֹדוֹת יָיִן

יִשְׁתַּחוּ אִישׁ וְיִשְׁכַּח רֵישׁוֹ לֹא יִזְכֹּר מְרִירוּת נַפְשׁוֹ
עָלָיו מִצְנָה לְהַקְדִּישׁוֹ מְאֹד נָאֶה קִדּוּשׁ יַיִן

עֲלֵה אָחִי בְּתוֹךְ גַּנִּי לִרְעוֹת לִשְׁתּוֹת יַיִן גַּפְנִי
יַחַד נָשִׁיר אַתָּה וַאֲנִי רַבִּים הֵמָּה שִׁירַת יַיִן

עִמְּךָ אֲשֶׁר בְּצֵל אוֹיְבִי וְלֹא תִשְׁתֶּה יַיִן הַרְבֵּה
כִּיכְרוֹב שֶׁמֶן הַנֵּר יִכְבֶּה כַּן הַרְבּוֹת שְׁתוֹת יָיִן

קוֹל דּוֹדִי הִנֵּה זֶה בָּא בְּרֹב אַהֲבָה וּבְרֹב חִבָּה
וְלֹא נִשְׁאַר בַּלֵּב אַבָּה וְשָׁלוֹם הִיא מִשְׁתֵּה יַיִן

קֶשֶׁב אָחִי לְאִמְרֵי פִי וְיֶעֱרַב לְךָ שִׁיר צַפְצוּפִי
וְהוּא כְּמוֹ נֹפֶת צוּפִי מְתוּקָה הִיא שְׁנַת יַיִן

בְּלֵיל שַׁבָּת מְאֹד מִצְוָה לִשְׁתּוֹת יַיִן כַּאֲשֶׁר צִוָּה
אֵלִי צוּרִי מִשְׁכָּן אָנָּה עוֹלַת מִנְחָה נֶסֶךְ יַיִן

בְּיוֹם שַׁבָּת קִדּוּשׁ וְהַבְדָּלָה וְאֶבָרֵךְ לְאֵל נַעֲלָה
וְאַהֲלְלָה יוֹם וָלַיְלָה יִפְתַּח לָנוּ אוֹצְרוֹת יַיִן

Jewish children, Samarkand.
Photo by S.M. Dudin, 1902.
(Russian Museum of Ethnography)

Notes

1. S. Weisenberg, 'Jews in Turkestan', in: *Jewish Past* Vol 5 (1912) p. 390. (In Russian)
2. V.V. Bartold, *Cultural History of Tajikistan* (Leningrad 1927) p. 47-48. (In Russian)
3. The only special collection in Central Asia was the Local Jewish Museum, founded in Samarkand in 1927 by an ethnographer I.S. Lurie. In 1934 the museum was closed down, and the collection distributed to other museums (in Samarkand, Tashkent, Dushanbe) and is now partially lost.
4. A. Dmitriev-Mamonov, *Guide to Turkestan and Tashkent and Central Asia Railroads* (St Petersburg 1903) p. 60. (In Russian)
5. A.M. Razgon, 'Russian History Museum. History of Foundation and Activities, 1872-1927', in: *Russian Museums History Survey* (Moscow 1960) p. 234. (In Russian)
6. After the exhibition the collections were passed over to Moscow Polytechnic Museum, and in 1902 were incorporated in the Dashkov Museum, founded in 1867 as the Department of Ethnic Studies of Moscow Public Rumyantsev Museum. See: *50 Years of Rumyantsev Museum in Moscow, 1862-1912. History Survey* (Moscow 1913) p. 168, 169, 173. (In Russian)
7. The Russian Museum of Ethnography (RME) was founded in 1895. It started as the Department of Ethnography of the Russian Museum of Alexander III, and became independent in 1934.
8. A.P. Fedchenko, *Collected Documents* (Tashkent 1956) p. 41-44. (In Russian)
9. *Ibid.* p. 164, 168. Because of the important part played by K. Kaufman in compiling the Turkestan collections for the Polytechnic exhibition, they are known as the Kaufman Collection. (In Russian)
10. RME Archives, F. 5, Inv. no. 4, File 36, p. 70. (In Russian)
11. O.A. Sukhareva, *History of Central Asian Dress. Samarkand (Second Half of Nineteenth - Early Twentieth Century)* (Moscow 1982) p. 26. (In Russian)
12. Territorial expansion of the Turkestan governorship continued until 1880, with the incorporation of part of the Bukharan Emirate and Turkmenistan.
13. M.M. Abramov, *Bukharan Jews in Samarkand, 1843-1917* (Samarkand 1993) p. 6, 7. (In Russian)
14. L.M. Kantor, *Local Jews in Uzbekistan* (Samarkand-Tashkent 1929) p. 6. (In Russian)
15. V.V. Krestovsky, *Visiting the Emir of Bukhara* (St Petersburg 1887) p. 189, 273. (In Russian)
16. S. Weisenberg, *op. cit.*, p. 403. (In Russian)
17. V.V. Krestovsky, *op. cit.* Moslems wear a belt on the under gown, except on certain occasions, such as during mourning.
18. *Ibid.*, p. 273.
19. *Ibid.*, p. 189, 272.
20. As a scientific employee of the Museum of Ethnography, Preobragensky worked in the Central Asian department. In 1926 he travelled to Central Asia to study Tajik ethnography. Among the many objects he collected were items relating to the Jews of Samarkand.
21. O.A. Sukhareva, *op. cit.*, p. 34, 35.
22. RME Archives, F. 5, Inv. no. 4, File 227, p. 1, 2.
23. This is in accordance with notes by other scholars. See N.F. Mashkov, 'Small-scale (Handmade) Silk Weaving in Uzbekistan', in: *Central Asian Silk* (Tashkent 1928) 2,3 p. 237 (In Russian) and N. Tursunov, *Urban Crafts in Northern Tajikistan (Weaving in Khodzhent and Suburbs in Late Nineteenth - Early Twentieth Century)* (Dushanbe 1974) p. 89. (In Russian)
24. RME Archives, F. 5, Inv. no. 4, File 227, p. 1, 2.
25. O.A. Sukhareva, *op. cit.*, p. 34-36.
26. S. Weisenberg, *op. cit.*, p. 400, 401.
27. *Ibid.*, p. 394.
28. RME Archives, F. 5, Inv. no. 4, File 227, p. 2.
29. RME Archives, F. 5, Inv. no. 4, File 227, p. 5-8.
30. The first Central Asian printing house with Hebrew alphabet was opened in 1910 in Kokand.
31. M.M. Abramov, *op. cit.*, p. 36.
32. Following his involvement in 1895 on the Archaeological committee of the Museum of Anthropology and Ethnography, and the Russian committee on Central and Eastern Asia, Dudin graduated in 1898 at the Academy of Art. As an artist, ethnographer and photographer he made three trips in the years 1900 to 1902 to Central Asia on behalf of the Ethnography Department of the Russian Museum in St Petersburg, the objects and photos he collected form the basis of the Museum's present Central Asian ethnography collection. In 1914 he was appointed scientific curator of the East and West Turkestan Antiquities Department of the Museum of Anthropology and Ethnography.
33. Weaving in Samarkand was a speciality of the Tajiks. In late nineteenth century Samarkand was the only area where serge cloth was made. In most local centres canvas or satin-type cloth still remained the most typical.
34. RME Archives, F. 5, Inv. no. 4, File 247, p. 156.
35. J.I. Kalontarov, 'Central Asian Jews', in: *Nations of Central Asia and Kazakhstan*, Vol.1. (Moscow 1963) p. 614, 615. (In Russian)
36. L.A. Chvyr, *Tajik Jewellery* (Moscow 1977) p. 86, 87. (In Russian)
37. This is explained not as much by the cost of gold, as by the belief that gold is the gift of Allah and should be handled only by the most pious.
38. The aim of the trip was to study the Moslem population of Bukhara, but as traditional cultural objects were mostly found in the old part of the city, where Bukharan Jews also reside, contact with the latter was unavoidable.
39. S. Weisenberg, *op. cit.*, p. 400, 401.
40. O.A. Sukhareva, *op. cit.*, p. 81, 82.
41. As with the main collection, the photography section comprised pieces acquired in 1948 from the Moscow Museum of Nations of the USSR, as well as those purchased by the Russian Museum of Ethnography.

CATALOGUE
Jews of Central Asia

INTRODUCTION

Bukharan Jews are a sub-ethnic Jewish group residing mostly in Central Asia, in the towns of Uzbekistan and the adjacent republics, as well as in Russia, Israel and the United States. The name comes from the Bukharan Emirate, a former feudal Moslem state in the territory of today's Uzbekistan and named after the capital, the city of Bukhara.

The Bukharan Jews speak Judeo-Tajic, a language related to Persian. This is a dialect of the Tajik language which is spoken in the area between the Syrdar'ya and the Amudar'ya rivers.

No definitive statistics are available on the Bukharan Jews, as the statistical data on the Jewish population of Central Asia and the Caucasus are largely approximations. In the mid-nineteenth century, Bukharan Jews in Central Asia numbered around 10,000. The population increased to *c.* 16,000 at the turn of the twentieth century and to 20,000 in the 1910s. Despite the massive *aliyah* in the 1970s, the population of *c.* 30,000 Bukharan Jews in Central Asia remained stable because of the high birth rate in the 1960s and 1970s. In the past decade, massive emigration by Bukharan Jews to Israel and the United States has considerably decreased the numbers living in their traditional surroundings. Certain communities of Bukharan Jews have even disintegrated (like those of Andizhan and Namangan, which had once been large). Unfortunately, no current statistics are available.

The largest communities of Bukharan Jews in Uzbekistan were located in Samarkand, Tashkent (capital of Uzbekistan), Bukhara, Shakhrisabz, Kattakurgan, Karmana, Khatyrchi, as well as in the cities of the Fergana Valley, such as Kokand, Margilan, Fergana, Andizhan, Namangan, Khodzhent (Tajikistan), Osh and Dzhalal-Abad (Kirgistan). In addition, Dushanbe, the capital of Tajikistan, used to have a large community of Bukharan Jews.

Jews are known to have lived in Central Asia since the Achaemenid period in Iran. Throughout the Middle Ages, the Jewish population was repeatedly documented in this area, the centre of ancient civilizations and part of the Great Silk Road. But both Bukharan and Afghani Jews drifted away from the overall Jewish population of Khorasan (Eastern Iran) rather late. This process, which began in the sixteenth and continued until the eighteenth century, severed contacts between the Jews of Eastern Iran and those of Central Asia. Bukharan Jews therefore represent one of the most recent sub-ethnic groups of all the Jewish communities. The full cycle of ethnogenesis (i.e. the

previous page
Tillay-ay (Jewish woman), from the picture album *Ethnic Types of the Turkestan area*, 1870s.
(Russian Museum of Ethnography)

separation of Bukharan Jews from their Iranian and Afghan counterparts) has not been completed, as the resemblances between ritual art from synagogues in Central Asia, Iran and Afghanistan indicate.

In the sixteenth century the first Jewish quarter, known as the Old *Mahalla*, was founded. In 1843 the Bukharan Emir sold the Jews a plot of land in Samarkand for a new Jewish quarter. This quarter, now called Vostok, still exists today and is the largest traditional Jewish quarter remaining in Central Asia.

A Jewish *mahalla* (quarter) is an integral part of many cities in Central Asia. In addition to those in Bukhara (where three adjacent quarters date back to the sixteenth to nineteenth centuries) and Samarkand, *mahallas* still exist in Shakhrisabz, Kattakurgan, Karmana, Kokand and Margilan.

Life in a compact and nationally homogeneous quarter guarantees all families support from their neighbours and safety, which has become more important in recent years; it also ensures continuity of religious traditions. The population of a Jewish quarter conforms to a hierarchy based on families and clans. Thus, a family from Samarkand has a higher status than one from Shakhrisabz. This is important in matchmaking. Even today, communal and family traditions largely determine the life of Bukharan Jews. A *shammash* in Margilan told us that his father had held the position before him. After his father's death, he had followed the decision of the Jewish community and resigned from his job as an engineer at the weaving factory to become the *shammash*. Endless joint celebrations strengthen local ties: commemorative ceremonies, engagements, weddings, circumcisions.

The community has an elected secular leader, known as the *kalantar*. Previously, the *kalantar* served as a judge and as the community's representative before the gentile authorities. Today this individual is primarily the religious head of the Jewish community and supervises the synagogue and the quarter's self-government. His main concerns are maintenance and upkeep. A *hakham* used to be the religious leader of a Jewish community (the equivalent of a rabbi in an Ashkenazi community). The last local *hakham* died in the early 1980s. Today, a *shohet* or *kalantar* retains sole responsibility for the community. New rabbis - educated in *yeshivas*, some from Israel - are arriving. The *Habad* movement has also achieved a considerable impact on the synagogues in Central Asia.

Bukharan Jews tend to follow all the life cycle rituals of circumcision, weddings and funerals. Observance of other religious rituals depends largely on the city, whether there is a Jewish *mahalla*, and whether the individual concerned lives in the *mahalla* or in a modern apartment complex. Nevertheless, Bukharan Jews are generally involved in religious activities. Most Jewish communities - even fairly small ones - have a *minyan* in the synagogue every morning.

The history of the Margilan synagogue illustrates the devotion of Bukharan Jews to their culture. In the 1930s the synagogue was closed and the building confiscated. The Jews of Margilan struggled until the end of the Second World War for permission to build a new synagogue. Raising funds and purchasing a plot of land took several years. Construction began in the winter of 1952-53. This effort is amazing, given the contemporary situation in the Soviet Union. While the Doctors' Trial was in full swing in Moscow, the Jewish community of Margilan was about to build a new synagogue, which remains active today.

In conservative societies small ethnic groups normally monopolize certain trades. Thus, Bukharan Jews are primarily involved in two trades: dyeing cloth (in the nineteenth century Jews were identified by their indigo-stained hands) and music. Even in the days of the Emir, Bukharan Jews were renowned for their skills as musicians, singers and manufacturers of musical instruments. Jewish musicians played at every Tajik or Uzbek wedding. Even today, many skilled performers of folk music from Central Asia are Bukharan Jews.

When factory-made fabrics appeared on the market, most dyers lost their jobs and had to change their line of work. Many Bukharan Jews became independent craftsmen, such as street cobblers, hairdressers, peddlers and the like. Under the Soviet Union, especially after the termination of the New Economic Policy, many Bukharan Jews worked in industries, while some entered the professions.

In terms of dress - specifically after the humiliating restrictions were abolished - cooking and housing, Bukharan Jews differ little from Moslems in Central Asia. In fact, the main difference between a traditional Moslem house and one owned by a Bukharan Jew is that the dwellings occupied by Jews do not have separate sections for men and women. In both Moslem and Jewish neighbourhoods, houses do not normally face the street. A Jewish *mahalla* is a labyrinth of intertwining streets with blank stone walls containing nothing but narrow gates, much like an old Moslem quarter. Past the gate is a large paved courtyard, followed by the façade of the house. Central Asian houses typically feature a large gallery-style terrace, or *aivan*, with decorative wooden columns supporting the roof. Homes are divided into summer and winter sections. The service areas are adjacent to the courtyard. In the mansions previously owned by wealthy Jewish Samarkand and Bukharan merchants, the most decorative room, known as the gala hall and also used as the family synagogue, has been preserved. The walls and the ceilings of these halls are decorated with wood carvings and *gunch*, colourful paintings and quotations from the Bible. Many of the interiors of such homes are masterpieces of Oriental art.

Bukharan synagogues are no different from Jewish residences. Located in the heart of the Jewish quarter, most Bukharan synagogues are homes converted for this purpose in the twentieth century. There are only two older synagogues: that of Bukhara, which was built more than 250 years ago, and the only cupola synagogue, Gumbaz synagogue (meaning dome), which was built in Samarkand in 1891. Most synagogues, like private houses, have an *aivan* that is used for prayers in the summer. Sometimes several prayer halls are located in the synagogue's courtyard (in Margilan the synagogue complex consists of two courtyards and three halls), as well as a *mikveh*, a hall for special community events, a room for *shehitah*, a *tandyr* (a traditional oven used in Central Asia for baking flat breads) for *mazzah* and a *sukkah* frame for Sukkot. The actual synagogue is a relatively small room that is almost square. As a rule, the *parokhot*, which cover the entire wall are the only decorations. They are red, green or lilac strips of velvet with inscriptions in Tajik or Hebrew in gold paint stating the date of death of the person in whose memory the *parokhet* was donated to the synagogue. The *parokhot* cover the entire wall, barely revealing the *Hekhal*. The *tevah* is located in the centre of the room or shifted towards the *Hekhal*. *Tevah* banisters are sometimes decorated with *rimmonim*. Long benches covered with cotton upholstery and tables with small cloth fans and *piales* for green tea, as well as prayer books, line the walls. The synagogues have a home-like and cosy feel.

The synagogues of Bukharan Jews contain a wonderful assortment of ritual items. Most date to the end of the nineteenth century, although some were made more recently. Many items are donations, following an ongoing tradition of commemorating deceased loved ones. Examples include a pair of *rimmonim* made of two metal Indian vases turned upside down and purchased at a local shop and a *kulmos* (pointer) chiselled from a silver spoon or a surgical knife. Bukharan Jewish communities have many 'secondary Judaica' items. For example, a Russian silver coffee cup is used as a *kiddush* cup and an Uzbek *suzani* (a cloth embroidered in the traditional Central Asian style) as a *parokhet*.

Silver *rimmonim* are of various styles and origins: local, Persian, Afghan, Russian, Polish, Austrian, Caucasian. Most *kulmoses* are made of silver and are flat, carefully tracing a hand.

Another interesting ritual object is the wand of the Prophet Elijah, which is characteristic of Afghan Jewish communities and is used at circumcisions. This symbolizes Elijah's invisible presence during the ceremony. Leather whips in the synagogues are for flagellation at Yom Kippur. Other items include elaborate pewter *hanukkiot*. Most Bukharan synagogues contain virtually complete sets of ritual objects, quite remarkable compared to the synagogues of other Jewish communities in the former Soviet republics.

Systematic studies of Bukharan Jewish culture were initiated rather late. In 1922 the ethnographer I.S. Lurie of St Petersburg travelled to Samarkand to collect items from Bukharan Jewish culture. The Museum of Indigenous Jews, based on this collection, was opened in the Jewish quarter of Samarkand in 1927. In 1931 Lurie, the museum's founder, was dismissed on ideological grounds and the museum converted into the Department of Indigenous Jews in the Samarkand Municipal Museum. In 1938 the department was closed and the collection transferred to the repositories of the Samarkand Museum. The archives, the collection of photographs and some 50 items from the Museum of Indigenous Jews remain there. The rest of the collection has been scattered.

Valery Dymshits

1. 8762-33767
Hat
Hats of this shape were compulsory for Jewish men in the late 19th - early 20th century in the Bukharan Emirate.
Fur, cotton, height 14.5 cm, diam. 29.5 cm
Samarkand, 1880-1910
From: Samarkand, 1880-1910
Purchased by S.P. Preobragensky in 1926 for the Museum of Ethnic Studies in Moscow; transferred to the RME in 1948

2. 8762-33769
Skull cap
Cotton, height 13 cm, diam. 23.5 cm
Samarkand, 1880-1910
From: Samarkand, 1880-1910
Purchased by S.P. Preobragensky in 1926 for the Museum of Ethnic Studies in Moscow; transferred to the RME in 1948

3. 8762-23963
Munisak
Gowns of this cut were worn by Moslem and Jewish women, as ritual garments; in the Jewish communities it was worn indoors by relatives of a deceased person during the seven days of mourning.
Silk, cotton, hand woven, 178 x 128 cm
Bukhara, 1880-1910
From: Samarkand, 1880-1910
Purchased by S.P. Preobragensky in 1926 for the Museum of Ethnic Studies in Moscow; transferred to the RME in 1948

4. 8762-33771
Tallit katan (beged)
Cotton, 46 x 31 cm
Palestine (?), late 19th - early 20th century
From: Samarkand, late 19th - early 20th century
Purchased by S.P. Preobragensky in 1926 for the Museum of Ethnic Studies in Moscow; transferred to the RME in 1948

5. 8761-13783/1,2
Tefillin
Leather, wood, sides 2.5 and 2.3 cm; strap length 260 and 325 cm
Palestine, late 19th - early 20th century
From: Samarkand, late 19th - early 20th century
Purchased by S.P. Preobragensky in 1926 for the Museum of Ethnic Studies in Moscow; transferred to the RME in 1948

6. 8761-13784/1,2
Tefillin cases
Cardboard, sides 7.2 cm
Palestine, late 19th - early 20th century
From: Samarkand, late 19th - early 20th century
Purchased by S.P. Preobragensky in 1926 for the Museum of Ethnic Studies in Moscow; transferred to the RME in 1948

7. 8762-33772
Tefillin bag
Decorated with gold embroidery featuring Jewish symbols and inscriptions, Yiddish on one side, Hebrew on the other, possibly the name of the owner: Moshe, son of the late Avraham Binyamin, 1893.
Velveteen, gold thread, 21 x 17.5 cm
Russia, late 19th century
From: Samarkand, late 19th - early 20th century
Purchased by S.P. Preobragensky in 1926 for the Museum of Ethnic Studies in Moscow; transferred to the RME in 1948

8. 8762-33773/1
Tefillin bag
Silk, cotton, 20 x 14 cm
Samarkand, 1880-1910
From: Samarkand, 1880-1910
Purchased by S.P. Preobragensky in 1926 for the Museum of Ethnic Studies in Moscow; transferred to the RME in 1948

9. 8762-3373/2
Mezuzah
Parchment, 11.5 x 11.5 cm
Palestine, 1870-1880
From: Samarkand, 1880-1920
Purchased by S.P. Preobragensky in 1926 for the Museum of Ethnic Studies in Moscow; transferred to the RME in 1948

10. 8762-33773/3
Komsa
Amulet against evil spirits with quotations from the Bible, normally rolled up and worn under the clothes in a bag or wrapped in a piece of cloth sewn on a garment.
Paper, 167 x 5.5 cm
Central Asia (Samarkand?), 1870-1880s
From: Samarkand, 1880-1920s
Purchased by S.P. Preobragensky in 1926 for the Museum of Ethnic Studies in Moscow; transferred to the RME in 1948

11. 8762-33773/4
Komsa
Fertility amulet with quotations from the Bible, normally rolled up and worn under the clothes in a bag or wrapped in a piece of cloth sewn on a garment.
Parchment, 20 x 7 cm
Palestine, 1870-1880s
From: Samarkand, 1880-1920s
Purchased by S.P. Preobragensky in 1926 for Museum of Ethnic Studies in Moscow; transferred to the RME in 1948

12. 8762-33773/5
Komsa
Amulet against impurity and unpleasantness with quotations from the Bible, normally rolled up and worn under the clothes in a bag or wrapped in a piece of cloth sewn on a garment.
Parchment, 32 x 8 cm
Palestine, 1870-1880s
From: Samarkand, 1880-1920s
Purchased by S.P. Preobragensky in 1926 for the Museum of Ethnic Studies in Moscow; transferred to the RME in 1948

13. 8762-33773/12
Komsa
Amulet against the evil eye, disease and decay with quotations from the Bible, normally rolled up and worn under the clothes in a bag or wrapped in a piece of cloth sewn on a garment.
Parchment, 41 x 7.5 cm
Palestine, 1870-1880s
From: Samarkand, 1880-1920s
Purchased by S.P. Preobragensky in 1926 for the Museum of Ethnic Studies in Moscow; transferred to the RME in 1948

14. 8762-33773/6
Chordevoli
Amulet with quotations from the Bible and Cabalistic formulas, hung on the four walls of the delivery room.
Parchment, 6 x 6.5 cm
Palestine, 1870-1880s
From: Samarkand, 1880-1920s
Purchased by S.P. Preobragensky in 1926 for the Museum of Ethnic Studies in Moscow; transferred to the RME in 1948

15. 8762-33773/11
Chordevoli
Amulet for mother and child against the evil eye with quotations from the Bible and Cabalistic formulas, hung on the four walls of the delivery room.
Paper, 24.8 x 17.5 cm
Palestine, 1870-1880s
From: Samarkand, 1880-1920s
Purchased by S.P. Preobragensky in 1926 for the Museum of Ethnic Studies in Moscow; transferred to the RME in 1948

16. 8762-33773/7
Mioro
Shivviti amulet with quotations from the Bible.
Parchment, 10 x 16 cm
Palestine, 1870-1880s
From: Samarkand, 1880-1920s
Purchased by S.P. Preobragensky in 1926 for the Museum of Ethnic Studies in Moscow; transferred to the RME in 1948

17. 8762-33773/8
Chordevoli
Amulet to protect mother and child with quotations from the Bible, hung on the wall of the delivery room.
Paper, max 10.5 x 8.3 cm
Palestine, 1870-1880s
From: Samarkand, 1880-1920s
Purchased by S.P. Preobragensky in 1926 for the Museum of Ethnic Studies in Moscow; transferred to the RME in 1948

18. 8762-33773/9
New Year greeting card
Card for the High Holidays in which the name was added in the blank space at the bottom.
Paper, lithographic print, 30 x 22 cm
Palestine, late 19 - early 20th century
From: Samarkand, late 19th - early 20th century
Purchased by S.P. Preobragensky in 1926 for the Museum of Ethnic Studies in Moscow; transferred to the RME in 1948

19. 8762-33773/10
Letter
Request for donations from *Misgav Ladach* hospital in Jerusalem, specially designed with letter head for Central Asia.
Paper, 23.6 x 15 cm
Jerusalem, late 19th - early 20th century
From: Samarkand, late 19th - early 20th century
Purchased by S.P. Preobragensky in 1926 for the Museum of Ethnic Studies in Moscow; transferred to the RME in 1948

20-25.
Man's costume
Late 1860s
Purchased in Samarkand in 1869 specifically for the All Russian Polytechnic Exhibition in Moscow in 1872 where it was listed as a 'Mannequin of a Turkestan Jew', this costume was acquired by the RME in 1948 from the former Museum of the Peoples of the USSR in Moscow.

20. 8762-33763
Under gown
Cotton, hand woven, length 117 cm, sleeve 83 cm, shoulders 54 cm
Samarkand, 1868-69

21. 8762-33764
Outer gown
Semi-silk, cotton, hand woven, length 148 cm, sleeve 96 cm, shoulder 43.5 cm
Samarkand, 1868-69

22. 8762-33765
Belt
Cotton, hand woven, 316 x 53 cm
Samarkand, 1868-69

23. 8762-33766
Hat
Velvet, cotton, fur, hand woven, height 21 cm, diam. 31 cm
Samarkand, 1868-69

24. 8762-33768
Skull cap
Silk, cotton, hair, hand woven, height 14 cm, diam. 25.5 cm
Samarkand, 1868-69

25. 8762-33770/1,2
Boots
Leather, 26 x 8 x 44 cm
Samarkand, 1868-69

26. 8762-23985
Man's hat
Shown at the All Russian Polytechnic Exhibition in Moscow in 1872.
Fur, cotton, height 20 cm, diam. 28 cm
Samarkand, 1868-69
From: Samarkand, 1869
Purchased specially for the All Russian Polytechnic Exhibition of 1872; transferred to the RME from the Moscow Museum of Ethnic Studies in 1948

27. 31-67/1,2
Poncha
Bracelets, noted in his inventory by the collector as '... worn by Jewish and Gypsy women, manufactured by Samarkand Sartes'.
Silver, coral, stamped, length pendant 1.2 cm, weight 64 grams
Samarkand, late 19th century
From: Samarkand, 1900-02
Purchased by S.M. Dudin in 1900-02 during an EDRM field trip to Central Asia

28. 31-107
Tavk
Necklace noted in his inventory by the collector as '...worn around the neck by rich Sarte and Jewish women'.
Gilt metal foil, coloured glass, pearls tourmalines (?), coral, stamped, faceted, 33 x 8 cm
Bukhara, late 19th century
From: Samarkand, 1900-02
Purchased by S.M. Dudin in 1900-02 during an EDRM field trip to Central Asia

29. 31-68
Kulutapushak
Woman's cap with pouch to contain hair, worn by married women, covered with one or more shawls, silk-embroidered with *iroqui* Shakhrisabz workmanship.
Cotton, silk thread, length pouch 33 cm, diam. 26 cm
Shakhrisabz, late 19th century
From: Samarkand, 1900-02
Purchased by S.M. Dudin in 1900-02 during an EDRM field trip to Central Asia

30. 31-104
Kulutapushak
Woman's cap with pouch to contain hair, worn by married women, covered with one or more shawls, silk-embroidered with *iroqui* Shakhrisabz workmanship.
Cotton, silk thread, length pouch 35 cm, diam. 26 cm
Shakhrisabz, late 19th century

From: Samarkand, 1900-02
Purchased by S.M. Dudin in 1900-02 during an EDRM field trip to Central Asia

31. 58-286
Kulutapushak
Woman's cap with pouch to contain hair, worn by married women, covered with one or more shawls, silk-embroidered with *iroqui* Shakhrisabz workmanship.
Cotton, silk thread, length pouch 36 cm, diam. 27 cm
Shakhrisabz, late 19th century
From: Samarkand, 1900-02
Purchased by S.M. Dudin in 1900-02 during an EDRM field trip to Central Asia

32. 58-287
Kulutapushak
Woman's cap with pouch to contain hair, worn by married women, covered with one or more shawls, silk-embroidered with *iroqui* Shakhrisabz workmanship.
Cotton, silk thread, length pouch 37 cm, diam. 29 cm
Shakhrisabz, late 19th century
From: Samarkand, 1900-02
Purchased by S.M. Dudin in 1900-02 during an EDRM field trip to Central Asia

33. 59-22
Kulutapushak
Gold-embroidered woman's cap with pouch to contain hair, worn by married women, covered with one or more shawls.
Velvet, cotton thread, metal thread, spangles, length pouch 38 cm, diam. 17 cm

Bukhara, late 19th century
From: Bukhara, 1900-02
Purchased by S.M. Dudin in 1900-02 during an EDRM field trip to Central Asia

34. 58-212
Tallit
Silk, hand woven, 207 x 160 cm
Samarkand, late 19th century
From: Samarkand, 1900-02
Purchased by S.M. Dudin in 1900-02 during an EDRM field trip to Central Asia

35. 11048-1
Woman's bracelet
Hinge fastener. Companion piece to no. 36.
Gold, punched, width 3.4 cm, diam. 9 cm, weight 70.2 grams
Bukhara, late 19th – early 20th century
From: Bukhara, late 19th – early 20th century
Purchased in 1988 in St Petersburg from a private owner

36. 11048-2
Woman's bracelet
Hinge fastener. Companion piece to no. 35.
Gold, punched, width 3.4 cm, diam. 6 cm, weight 56 grams
Bukhara, late 19th – early 20th century
From: Bukhara, late 19th – early 20th century
Purchased in 1988 in St Petersburg from a private owner

37. 11079-10
Sarband
Woman's shawl of tulle, decorated with spangles, popular among young Jewish women and worn over caps (no. 53), head bands (nos 54, 55, 56) or over another shawl.
Cotton, metal spangles, spangle embroidery, length diagonal 270 cm, length sides 200 cm
Iran (?), late 19th – early 20th century
From: Bukhara, late 19th – early 20th century
Purchased by T. Emelyanenko in 1988 during a RME field trip to Central Asia

38. 11596-1
Dress
Type of open tunic of manufactured cloth with stand-up collar that spread to Central Asia in the 1880s, mostly among the urban population of the Fergana Valley and Tashkent.
Silk, 127 x 92 cm
Margilan, early 20th century
From: Margilan, early 20th century
Purchased in 1994 in St Petersburg from a private owner

39. 11596-2
Dress
Type of open tunic of manufactured cloth with stand-up collar that spread to Central Asia in the 1880s, mostly among the urban population of the Fergana Valley and Tashkent.
Silk, 130 x 105 cm
Margilan, early 20th century
From: Margilan, early 20th century
Purchased in 1994 in St Petersburg from a private owner

40. 11631-1
Torah scroll case
Patterned velvet, wood, metal, height 54 cm, diam. 24 cm
Eastern Europe (?), 19th century
From: Kokand, 19th – early 20th century
Purchased by the St Petersburg Jewish University staff in Kokand in 1993. Donated to the RME in 1994

Girl's cap, Bukhara
(cat. no. 53)

Pieces collected by V.V. Kucherov on behalf of the Russian Museum of Ethnography in 1995-1996 and shown as items from the private collection of V.V. Kucherov.

41. BX149
Dress
Made of handmade *shoyi* silk from Bukhara, with *ikat* decoration *(abr* in Uzbek and Tajik).
Silk, hand woven, 121 x 100 cm
Bukhara, late 19th - early 20th century
From: Bukhara, late 19th - early 20th century
Private collection of V.V. Kucherov

42. BX150
Dress
Made of handmade *shoyi* silk from Bukhara, with *ikat* decoration *(abr* in Uzbek and Tajik).
Silk, hand woven, 121 x 100 cm
Bukhara, late 19th - early 20th century
From: Bukhara, late 19th - early 20th century
Private collection of V.V. Kucherov

43. BX151
Dress
Made of handmade *adras* semi-silk from Gizhduvan, with *ikat* decoration *(abr* in Uzbek and Tajik) and *peshkurta* band decorated with gold *guilduzi* embroidery (the outlines traced in embroidery) on the collar.
Semi-silk, velvet, metal thread, hand woven, 116 x 115 cm
Bukhara, late 19th - early 20th century
From: Bukhara, late 19th - early 20th century
Private collection of V.V. Kucherov

44. BX152
Dress
Made of handmade *adras* semi-silk from Gizhduvan, with *ikat* decoration *(abr* in Uzbek and Tajik) and *peshkurta* band decorated with gold *zaminduzi* embroidery (entirely covered with embroidery) on the collar.
Semi-silk, metal thread, metal, hand woven, 126 x 110 cm
Bukhara, late 19th - early 20th century
From: Bukhara, late 19th - early 20th century
Private collection of V.V. Kucherov

45. BX153
Dress
Made of handmade striped *bekasab* semi-silk from Kitab, with *ikat* decoration *(abr* in Uzbek and Tajik) and *peshkurta* band decorated with silk *iroqui* (semi-cross) embroidery on the collar; the band made in Shakhrisabz.
Semi-silk, silk thread, hand woven, 128 x 100 cm
Bukhara, late 19th - early 20th century
From: Bukhara, late 19th - early 20th century
Private collection of V.V. Kucherov

46. BX154
Dress
Made of handmade striped *alochaï karatagi* silk from Karatag, with *peshkurta* band decorated with silk *iroqui* (semi-cross) embroidery on the collar; the band made in Shakhrisabz.
Silk, silk thread, hand woven, 128 x 100 cm
Bukhara, late 19th - early 20th century
From: Bukhara, late 19th - early 20th century
Private collection of V.V. Kucherov

47. BX155
Dress
Made of handmade *shoyi* silk from Tashkent.
Silk, hand woven, 144 x 106 cm
Tashkent, late 19th - early 20th century
From: Tashkent, late 19th - early 20th century
Private collection of V.V. Kucherov

48. BX156
Dress
Worn on Yom Kippur.
Guipure, 134 x 107 cm
Kokand, early 20th century
From: Kokand, early 20th century
Private collection of V.V. Kucherov

49. BX158
Woman's gown
Differing from the traditional tunic cut, this woman's gown made of patterned factory-made silk, stitched-in sleeves and shoulder seams became popular in Central Asia in 1880s, mostly among the urban population.
Silk, 135 x 150 cm
Bukhara, late 19th - early 20th century
From: Bukhara, late 19th - early 20th century
Private collection of V.V. Kucherov

50. BX159
Woman's gown
A new style of festive dress made in Bukhara in the early 20th century of patterned factory-made silk with stitched-in sleeves and shoulder seams which became popular in Central Asia in the late 19th century.
Silk, cotton, 116 x 36 cm
Bukhara, late 19th - early 20th century
From: Bukhara, late 19th - early 20th century
Private collection of V.V. Kucherov

51. BX160
Paranja
Made of factory-made velvet, trimmed with machine embroidery and hand-embroidered band.
Velvet, silk thread, 161 x 71 cm
Bukhara, late 19th - early 20th century
From: Bukhara, late 19th - early 20th century
Private collection of V.V. Kucherov

52. BX161
Kulutapushak
Woman's cap with pouch for hair, decorated with gold embroidery.
Velvet, metal thread, length pouch 35 cm, diam. 58 cm
Bukhara, late 19th - early 20th century
From: Bukhara, late 19th - early 20th century
Private collection of V.V. Kucherov

53. BX162
Woman's cap
Decorated with gold *zaminduzi* embroidery (entirely covered with embroidery) and worn by girls and young women as a separate festive headpiece or with a shawl.
Cotton, metal thread, height 11 cm, diam. 30 cm
Bukhara, late 19th - early 20th century
From: Bukhara, late 19th - early 20th century
Private collection of V.V. Kucherov

Family Seder on the veranda, or *aivan*, Samarkand, early 20th century.

The elders of Samarkand, *c.* 1911. (Indigenous Jewish Museum Collection, Municipal Museum, Samarkand)

54. BX163
Peshonaband
Young woman's forehead band decorated with gold embroidery.
Silk, metal thread, 10 x 53 cm
Bukhara, late 19th - early 20th century
From: Bukhara, late 19th - early 20th century
Private collection of V.V. Kucherov

55. BX164
Peshonaband
Young woman's forehead band decorated with gold embroidery.
Silk, metal thread, 11 x 57 cm
Bukhara, late 19th - early 20th century
From: Bukhara, late 19th - early 20th century
Private collection of V.V. Kucherov

56. BX165
Peshonaband
Young woman's forehead band decorated with gold embroidery.
Silk, metal thread, 9.8 x 5.4 cm
Bukhara, late 19th - early 20th century
From: Bukhara, late 19th - early 20th century
Private collection of V.V. Kucherov

57. BX166
Shawl
Triangular cloth of brocade, worn as an under shawl or forehead band as one of several scarves and shawls of a married woman's costume.
Brocade, max. side length 90 cm
Manufacturing unknown
From: Bukhara, first half of the 19th century
Private collection of V.V. Kucherov

58. BX170
Shawl
Manufactured in Russia in the first half of the 20th century, these shawls were exported extensively to Central Asia and worn by all the peoples of the area.
Silk, 80 x 114 cm
From: Tashkent
Private collection of V.V. Kucherov

59. BX174
Shawl
Manufactured in Russia in the first half of the 20th century, these shawls were exported extensively to Central Asia and worn by all the peoples of the area.
Silk, 120 x 120 cm
From: Tashkent
Private collection of V.V. Kucherov

60. BX175
Shawl
Manufactured in Russia in the first half of the 20th century, these shawls were exported extensively to Central Asia and worn by all the peoples of the area.
Silk, 122 x 118 cm
From: Tashkent
Private collection of V.V.Kucherov

61. BX177
Shawl
Manufactured in Russia in the first half of the 20th century, these shawls were exported extensively to Central Asia and worn by all the peoples of the area.
Silk, 106 x 108 cm
From: Tashkent
Private collection of V.V. Kucherov

62. BX180
Man's gown
Made of handmade striped semi-silk *alochai gissari* (woven in the Gissara valley, in today's Tajikistan) and decorated with hand-wattled ribbon, straight cut, shoulder seams and stitched-in sleeves.
Silk, cotton, 127 x 80 cm
Bukhara, late 19th - early 20th century
From: Bukhara, late 19th - early 20th century
Private collection of V.V. Kucherov

63. BX181
Nosi gardan
Breast ornament with a central medallion and four square plaques of stamped gold foil inlaid with mastic, connected with six rows of chains; silk lace at the ends.
Gold (585 and 958), pearls, almandine, beryl, coral, tourmaline, spinel, mastic, threads, stamped, faceted, length sides 29 cm, width max of central medallion 7 cm, side plaques 1.5 x 3.0 cm, weight 149.4 grams
Bukhara, late 19th - early 20th century
From: Bukhara, late 19th - early 20th century
Private collection of V.V. Kucherov

64. BX182
Woman's bracelet
Circular band of pierced gold plaque with filigree pattern and hinge fastener.
Gold (585), punched, 18.7 x 2.1 cm, diam. 5.8 cm, weight 36.32 grams
Bukhara, late 19th - early 20th century
From: Bukhara, late 19th - early 20th century
Private collection of V.V. Kucherov

65. BX183/1,2
Woman's earrings
Round base, with pendants of pearls and coloured stones.
Gold (500 and 750), pearl, beryl, tourmaline, printed, faceted, length 5.5 cm, diam. c. 2.5 cm, total weight 27.92 (14.01 and 13.91)
Bukhara, late 19th - early 20th century
From: Bukhara, late 19th - early 20th century
Private collection of V.V. Kucherov

66. BX187
Bowl
Decorated with engraved and chased foliate pattern, and Arabic inscriptions on the edge.
Bronze, cast, tinned, engraved, chased, height 16 cm, diam. 33.5 cm
Bukhara, late 19th century
From: Tashkent, late 19th - early 20th century
Private collection of V.V. Kucherov

67. BX188
Bowl
Copper, height 12 cm, diam. mouth 18 cm
Bukhara, early 20th century
From: Tashkent, early 20th century
Private collection of V.V. Kucherov

68. BX189
Ladle
Tin-plated copper, length handle 31 cm, diam. bowl 6 cm
Tashkent, early 20th century
From: Tashkent, early 20th century
Private collection of V.V. Kucherov

69. BX190
Ladle
Tin-plated copper, length handle 34 cm, diam. bowl 11 cm

Tashkent, early 20th century
From: Tashkent, early 20th century
Private collection of V.V. Kucherov

70. BX191/1,2
Pestle and mortar
Brass, cast, height mortar 12 cm, length pestle 25 cm
Manufacturing unknown
From: Tashkent, first half of the 20th century
Private collection of V.V. Kucherov

71. BX192
Tray
Tin-plated copper, cast, engraved, diam. 72 cm
Bukhara, early 20th century
From: Tashkent, early 20th century
Private collection of V.V. Kucherov

72. BX193
Tray
Tin-plated copper, cast, engraved, diam. 54 cm
Bukhara, early 20th century
From: Tashkent, early 20th century
Private collection of V.V. Kucherov

73. BX194
Tray
Tin-plated copper, cast, engraved, diam. 43 cm
Bukhara, early 20th century
From: Tashkent, early 20th century
Purchased in 1988 in St Petersburg from a private owner

74. BX195
Khum
Vessel for storing wine.
Earthenware, height 62 cm, diam. 55 cm, diam. neck 30 cm
Bukhara, late 19th - early 20th century
From: Tashkent, early 20th century
Private collection of V.V. Kucherov

75. BX196
Spiked mazzah rolling pin
Wood, metal, 36 cm
Tashkent, early 20th century
From: Tashkent, early 20th century
Private collection of V.V. Kucherov

76. BX197/1,2
Rimmonim
Silver (960), metal (hooks, bells, ringlets), 232.7 grams (1), 231.5 grams (2)
Eastern Europe (?), late 19th - early 20th century
From: Tashkent, early 20th century
Private collection of V.V. Kucherov

Tatjana Emelyanenko

Additional items from the Russian Museum of Ethnography Central Asia collection

77. 58-81
Chachvan
Horse hair, veil, ribbon, 93 x 60 cm
Samarkand, late 19th century
Tajik
S.M. Dudin, 1900-02

78. 58-85
Kerchief
Silk, 124 x 142 cm
Samarkand, late 19th century
Tajik
S.M. Dudin, 1900-02

79. 58-88b
Kerchief
Cotton, 133 x 130 cm
Samarkand, late 19th century
Tajik
S.M. Dudin, 1900-02

80. 60-2
Woman's dress
Silk, 144 x 77 cm
Kokand, late 19th century
Uzbek
S.M. Dudin, 1900-02

81. 60-22
Kerchief
Silk, 133 x 144 cm
Kokand, late 19th century
Uzbek
S.M. Dudin, 1900-02

82. 60-36
Cloth
Silk, 265 x 135 cm
Kokand, late 19th century
Uzbek
S.M. Dudin, 1900-02

83. 244-17
Jug
Earthenware, height 16.5 cm, diam. 11 cm
Bukhara, late 19th century
Tajik
S.M. Dudin, 1900-02

84. 244-43
Jug
Copper, brass, height 28.5 cm, diam. 10.5 cm
Bukhara, late 19th century
Tajik
S.M. Dudin, 1900-02

85. 244-101
Candlestick
Tin-plated copper, height 31 cm, diam. 30.5 cm
Bukhara, late 19th century
Tajik
S.M. Dudin, 1900-02

86. 362-20
Carpet
Wool, 240 x 182 cm
Samarkand, late 19th century
Uzbek
S.M. Dudin, 1900-02

87. 1162-1
Jug
Copper, brass, tin, height 30 cm, diam. 12.5 cm
Bukhara, late 19th century
Uzbek
Bought from a private owner in St Petersburg in 1906

88. 5549-27abc
Wash-stand
Copper, brass, tin, diam. 36 cm
Bukhara, late 19th century
Uzbek
Transferred from the State Museum Fund in 1923

89. 5549-51
Vessel for water
Copper, brass, tin, height 33 cm, diam. 10.5 cm
Bukhara, late 19th century
Uzbek
Transferred from the State Museum Fund in 1923

90. 6141-159
Shirt
Cotton, 69 x 46 cm
Uzbekistan, 1950s
Uzbek
Bought by M.V. Sazonova during an expedition of the RME in 1956

91. 6159-131
Printed fabric
Cotton, 158 x 115 cm
Uzbekistan, 1950s
Uzbek
Bought by V.G. Grigoriev during an expedition of the RME in 1957

92. 6772-21
Cloth
Cashmere, 160 x 134 cm
Late 19th century
Uzbek
Transferred from the State Museum Fund in 1923

93. 7121-33
Drinking cup
Porcelain, height 5.8 cm, diam 11.2 cm
Uzbekistan, 1960s
Uzbek
Bought by B.Z. Gamburg during an expedition of the RME in 1962

94. 7228-17
Vessel for water
Copper, brass, height 40 cm
Uzbekistan, late 19th century
Uzbek
Bought from a private owner in St Petersburg in 1965

95. 7380-15
Candlestick
Tin-plated copper, height 34.5 cm
Uzbekistan, late 19th century
Uzbek
Bought from a private owner in St Petersburg in 1965

96. 7609-30
Drinking cup
Porcelain, height 5 cm, diam. 11.2 cm
Uzbekistan, 1960s
Uzbek
Bought by B.Z. Gamburg during an expedition of the RME in 1966

97. 7609-117
Necklace
Coral, 59 cm
Uzbekistan, first half 20th century
Uzbek
Bought by B.Z. Gamburg during an expedition of the RME in 1966

98. 8171-149
Dish
Earthenware, diam. 29 cm
Uzbekistan, mid-20th century
Uzbek
Bought by B.Z. Gamburg during an expedition of the RME in 1972

99. 8519-1
Tray
Brass, diam. 36.5 cm
Uzbekistan, late 19th - early 20th century
Uzbek
Bought from a private owner in 1973

100. 8761-11552
Cage-spool
Wood, 54 x 44 cm
Uzbekistan, late 19th - early 20th century
Uzbek
Transferred from the Museum of Ethnic Studies in Moscow in 1948

101. 8761-12444
Dish
Earthenware, diam. 38 cm
Uzbekistan, early 20th century
Uzbek
Transferred from the Museum of Ethnic Studies in Moscow in 1948

102. 8761-12506
Bowl
Earthenware, diam. 18 cm
Uzbekistan, early 20th century
Uzbek
Transferred from the Museum of Ethnic Studies in Moscow in 1948

103. 8761-12514
Bowl
Porcelain, height 8 cm
Uzbekistan, early 20th century
Uzbek
Transferred from the Museum of Ethnic Studies in Moscow in 1948

104. 8761-13832
Chest
Wood, metal, 78 x 32 x 36 cm
Kirghizia, early 20th century
Kirghiz
Transferred from the Museum of Ethnic Studies in Moscow in 1948

105. 8762-20587
Robe
Semi-silk, 127 x 56 cm
Uzbekistan, late 19th - early 20th century
Uzbek
Transferred from the Museum of Ethnic Studies in Moscow in 1948

106. 8762-20937
Belt
Silk, 98 x 10 cm
Uzbekistan, late 19th - early 20th century
Uzbek
Transferred from the Museum of Ethnic Studies in Moscow in 1948

107. 8762-21205
Breast adornment
Gilt silver, coral, turquoise, 27 x 84 cm
Bukhara, late 19th - early 20th century
Uzbek
Transferred from the Museum of Ethnic Studies in Moscow in 1948

108. 8762-21829
Suzani
Embroidered cover.
Cotton, silk, 270 x 157 cm
Bukhara, late 19th - early 20th century
Uzbek
Transferred from the Museum of Ethnic Studies in Moscow in 1948

109. 8762-21830
Suzani
Curtain.
Cotton, silk, 241 x 165 cm
Bukhara, late 19th - early 20th century
Uzbek
Transferred from the Museum of Ethnic Studies in Moscow in 1948

110. 8762-21855
Rug
Cotton, semi-silk, 135 x 53 cm
Bukhara, late 19th - early 20th century

Uzbek
Transferred from the Museum of Ethnic Studies in Moscow in 1948

111. 8762-22018
Robe
Semi-silk, 142 x 209 cm
Bukhara, late 19th – early 20th century
Tajik
Transferred from the Museum of Ethnic Studies in Moscow in 1948

112. 8762-22324
Necklace
Coral, glass, 39 cm
Bukhara, late 19th – early 20th century
Tajik
Transferred from the Museum of Ethnic Studies in Moscow in 1948

113. 8762-23525
Skull cap
Silk, height 15 cm, diam. 55 cm
Kazakh, late 19th century
Transferred from the Museum of Ethnic Studies in Moscow in 1948

114. 8171-218
Jug
Earthenware, height 22 cm
Samarkand, late 19th – early 20th century
Tajik
Bought by B.Z. Gamburg during an expedition of the RME in 1976

115. 9924-1
Suzani
Wall embroidery.
Tashkent, late 19th – early 20th century
Uzbek
Bought from a private owner in St Petersburg in 1982

116. 10029-1ab
Teapot
Earthenware, height 12.5 cm
Uzbekistan, late 19th – early 20th century
Uzbek
Bought from a private owner in St Petersburg in 1991

117. 11206-4
Beads
Coral, glass, metal, 33 cm
Uzbekistan, late 19th – early 20th century
Uzbek
Bought by S.I. Ilushenko during an expedition of the RME in 1990

118. 11206-5
Beads
Coral, 40 cm
Uzbekistan, late 19th – early 20th century
Uzbek
Bought by S.I. Ilushenko during an expedition of the RME in 1990

119. 11661-1
Vessel for ablution
Brass, height 37 cm, diam. 54 cm
Bukhara, late 19th – early 20th century
Uzbek
Bought from a private owner in St Petersburg in 1994

120. 242-20
Belt
Leather, silver, turquoise, 107 x 8.8 cm
Bukhara, late 19th – early 20th century
Uzbek
S.M. Dudin, 1900-02

121. 10786-12
Breast decoration
Silver, coral, glass, 34 cm
Samarkand, late 19th – early 20th century
Tajik
Bought from a private owner in St Petersburg in 1990

122. 20-142
Plate
Earthenware, 6 cm, diam. 30.5 cm
Bukhara, late 19th century
Uzbek
S.M. Dudin, 1900-02

123. 20-149
Shawl
Silk, 222 x 99 cm
Bukhara, late 19th century
Uzbek
S.M. Dudin, 1900-02

124. 20-157
Scarf
Silk, 242 x 52 cm
Bukhara, late 19th century
Uzbek
S.M. Dudin, 1900-02

125. 22-68
Piola
Wine cup.
Brass, blue pasta inlay outside, silver inside, 12 cm, diam. 5.5 cm
Bukhara, late 19th century
Uzbek
S.M. Dudin, 1900-02

126. 26-24
Carpet
Wool, 142 x 112 cm
Turkmenistan, late 19th century
S.M. Dudin, 1900-02

127. 58-27
Kamzol
Man's coat.
Wool, cotton, bone, 100 x 47 cm
Samarkand, late 19th century
Tajik
S.M. Dudin, 1900-02

128. 58-49
Man's cap
Sheepskin, fur, height 22 cm
Samarkand, late 19th century
Tajik
S.M. Dudin, 1900-02

Street in the Jewish quarter of Samarkand. Photo by S.M. Dudin, 1902. (Russian Museum of Ethnography)

Mountain Jewish wedding, Kuba, late 19th century.
(Beth Hatefutsoth Photo Archive)

Jews of the Caucasus

Vladimir Dmitriev
Russian Museum of Ethnography, St Petersburg

Originally known as the Ethnography Department of the Russian Museum of Alexander III, the Russian Museum of Ethnography in St Petersburg has a relatively small collection of objects relating to the Jews of the Caucasus derived from a variety of sources, including the museum's own field trips, purchases from individuals and contributions from other museums. The principal contribution was made in 1948, when the bulk of the Moscow Museum of Ethnic Studies (Museum of Peoples of the USSR) collection was transferred to St Petersburg. Another significant contribution came when a number of items were brought over from the Museum of History and Ethnography of Georgian Jews. The St Petersburg collection offers an important, though incomplete, survey of the secular, and, to a lesser extent, religious culture of Eastern Caucasian Jews (the Tats) and Georgian Jews.

A deliberate and precise policy with regard to the collection of cultural material relating to the Caucasian Jews was never pursued in St Petersburg: there was no collection schedule, no structural plan. Even the manuscripts by I. Pulner,[1] an expert on Ashkenazi culture who described the lifestyle of the Georgian Jews in his student years (1926), did not change this.[2] Even so, Pulner's manuscript forms a valuable contribution to the cultural history of the Georgian Jews.

The Caucasian Jewish collection reflects the general principles on which the ethnographic examination of the Caucasian peoples is based at the museum and the various approaches to the formation of a collection. One of the reasons for the limited representation of each culture is the sheer number of Caucasian peoples and the limited availability of ethnographic scholars.

Both the collection policies of the museum's Caucasian department and the studies on Caucasian Jews can be divided into two periods: the early years, 1900-1925, and the main years, 1930-1970. The dominant feature of the early period was the attempt to create a comprehensive picture of a traditional Caucasian culture. Later, the emphasis was on the specific features of each people, based on the concept of an *ethnos* as a culturally unique entity. In line with the political circumstances of the day these activities were mainstreamed into the studies of those peoples that had their own administrative or government structures. The Jews, like many other minor peoples in the Caucasus,

HEBREW WEDDING SONG OF THE GEORGIAN JEWS

Hebrew wedding song, recorded by ethnographer I. Pulner, Oni, Georgia, 1928. (Russian Museum of Ethnography Archives, Pulner Archive F.9, Inv. no. 1, File 20, p.16) This is the first publication of an extract from Pulner's extensive manuscript (courtesy of RME).

Wedding Song
Sung when the bride and bridegroom enter after the Kiddush

Bridegroom, handsomest of men, and bride dressed in finery.
Bride, prettiest of women, and bridegroom dressed in finery.
The groom is handsome, his desire is great;
His bride is Eve, mother of all the House of Israel.
Abraham our father, handsomest of men, and Sarah (his bride) dressed in finery.
This bridegroom is a light that shines brightly;
His bride is like Sarah, the first of all Israel.
Sarah, prettiest of women, and bridegroom dressed in finery.
May many good things come to him without delay;
His bride is like Rachel who loved Israel (Jacob).
Jacob our father handsomest of men, and bride dressed in finery.
May the bridegroom be pleased with his bride, with every happiness and every joy and every gladness and cheer according to the laws of Israel.
The sound of joy and the sound of happiness,
The voice of the bridegroom and the voice of the bride.

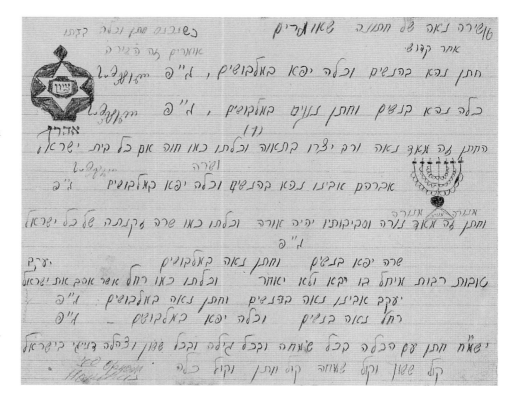

were not among these. Jewish objects continued to arrive at the museum, but less regularly. The early years were characterized by intensive field work; later, most of the contributions came from other museums or were purchased from individuals. Another obstacle was the idea that a museum should collect items with characteristic ethnic distinctions, while for Jews items of this kind had long been obsolete. Today these ideas, typical of 1960s ethnography, are considered outdated.

The first item acquired for the museum's Jewish collection dates from early 1903, the first year of the institution's activities. The piece purchased was an ornate costume of a Jewish woman from Akhaltsikh, in Georgia. But to start with Eastern Caucasia, in 1909 the famous scholar and Department of Ethnography curator A.A. Miller[3] travelled to Northern Azerbaijan. Having worked the previous year in Dagestan as well as in north and southwest Russian Azerbaijan, this was part of his attempt to complete a comprehensive study of the Caucasus. One of the aspects of the folk culture Miller studied was that of Eastern Caucasian carpets, which led him to the main carpet and craft centre of Northern Azerbaijan, the city of Kuba. Here, he gathered three separate collections: a large miscellaneous Azerbaijani collection, a collection of carpets made by Moslem Tats and a collection of articles belonging to the Mountain Jews of Krasnaya Sloboda on the outskirts of Kuba (collection No. 1735).

Miller defined Moslem Tats as Tats, and Jewish Tats as Jews. This definition highlights a lively dispute among Russian Caucasian scholars concerning the ethnic background of Dagestani and Northern Azerbaijani Tats. No account was taken in pre-revolutionary censuses of ethnic distinctions; only of religious persuasion. Most ethnographers of the period accepted this categorization. Studies by I. Cherny,[4] I.S. Anisimov,[5] Vs.S. Miller[6] focus on the culture of a group with a common religion – Judaism – and defined as Caucasian Jews, Mountain Jews or Dag Chu Fut (a Turkic name). With the advances in ethnology and linguistics in 1910s and 1920s, language became the main factor for defining an ethnic group. Caucasian scholars described the Tat language as part of the Iranian group: it was shown to be spoken by Moslems, Gregorian Christians and Jews alike. The language and habitat of the Tats were described by B. Miller.[7] Soviet ethnographers saw the ethnic groups primarily as social entities, united by factors such as territory, economy, language, psychology and religion. This led to a dual concept of the Tats' ethnic background. On the one hand, they were regarded as a people – the Tats[8] – on the other, the Tats and the Mountain Jews were treated as separate peoples.[9] Political issues complicated the situation even further: the Tats were declared to be one of the Dagestani peoples, which made it possible to discover the Mountain Jews in Azerbaijan.

In his report of 1909, A.A. Miller took a characteristically positivist line: describing actual pieces in actual places. The people of the Jewish district of Sloboda in Kuba were considered by their neighbours and by themselves, to be first and foremost Jews, and then Tats. With his report on his discoveries in Kuba, Miller contributed, consciously or unconsciously, to the dispute surrounding the economic status of the Mountain Jews. Before his research, they were thought to have been involved mainly in small-scale trade,[10] as well as agriculture, silk manufacture and leather processing.[11] According to Miller, the Mountain Jews of Kuba were involved exclusively in small-scale trading, and all their traditional items, including religious objects, were commissioned from Moslems.[12] Miller's description of the situation was probably accurate, yet his remarks deserve closer examination. A rich variety of crafts was practised in the Kuba area, and because of their diversity and the multicultural character of Northern Azerbaijan, each ethnic group specialized in a particular area. Meanwhile, Islamic and Turkic dominion of Eastern Caucasia had led to a change in ethnic identification. It is well known that in the late nineteenth century a folk memory still existed of a wider Jewish community, and many Turkic Moslems claimed to have had Jewish ancestors; this suggests that the ethnic exchange of the late nineteenth century followed the economic exchange of a previous period. Indeed, no professional restrictions applied to the Dag Chu Fut of the Eastern Caucasus, while Kuba, a former feudal principality, might have been expected to have been a place where the restrictive laws of the Moslem Orient would have applied.

Yet, certain items in collection No. 1735 cast doubt on Miller's remarks, notably a band-weaving loom used in silk workshops (cat. no. 45). The band was used for lifting water jugs – strictly a woman's job among the Caucasian peoples. The band was also used for belts in ordinary women's garments. A spindle (cat. no. 44) reveals that Jews were involved in weaving, or at least in making thread. Mountain Jewish women were therefore much like other Caucasian women; as the local saying went, 'if she has no spindle, she's probably

dying'. The position of the spindle is typically Asian – distaff upwards. Clearly, Miller was referring to men, who lived an outdoor life; women, with their secluded existence, apparently had more in common with the indigenous population.

Generally, women bought ready-made fabrics for most of their clothes; but apart from bands they also knitted their own socks. The presence of a wooden knitting last (cat. no. 40) in the collection is intriguing, since most traditional urban women did not use them. The socks, essential on the cold floors, had no specific decorative value.

Another women's occupation is represented by a rolling pin, a spatula and a board for making flat breads and placing these along the oven walls (cat. nos 42, 41, 43). This proves there were two types of oven: one for browning grain and baking bread in the ashes, and another for baking flat breads, on the clay walls of the oven. The spatula was used in the first type, and the board in the second. This combination of two types is typical for the border region of Transcaucasia and Northeast Caucasia.

Several items were used by children. A small wooden toboggan (cat. no. 46) with two runners and two bars was used in a popular boy's game, sliding downhill. Tobogganing is a favourite pastime in the Caucasus, one of the national sports. Young children, especially girls would play with dolls. There are no dolls in the collection, but there is a toy cradle (cat. no. 47). It is lifelike and detailed – a mattress, blankets, but no pillow. The doll would lie on its back, wrapped tightly in a blanket. Nevertheless, this rocking cradle is rather unusual for the Caucasus. Normally, a cradle would rock on a curved base. Here the base is flat, the upper bar is raised high with the main part suspended on ropes. It is not clear whether it represents a different type of cradle or whether it is a rough imitation.

Miller's collection includes women's garments and ornaments. No men's costumes were purchased: probably because they lacked any specific features. It is possible to obtain an idea of a Mountain Jew's garments from photographs in the museum archives. These show a typical male costume of Eastern Caucasia: a *beshmet* (shirt) with high collar and over this a *chukha* – an open knee-length garment with a tailored waistline, open neck and no collar. A leather or metal belt was worn with the *chukha*, on which a dagger was hung. Mountain Jews would naturally carry weapons, distinguishing them from other Oriental Jews. According to Anisimov, Eastern Caucasian Jews would leave their daggers at home only on Saturdays. It is worth noting that a Caucasian of any other people would probably have worn a far wider assortment of arms when posing for a photograph. Wearing a dagger is not a token of the militancy of the Mountain Jews; it is simply an accessory that all locals wore. In fact, the dagger was the most personal of all weapons in the Caucasus.[13]

Mountain Jewish musicians sending off a Jewish soldier leaving for the tsarist army, Kuba, 1896. (Beth Hatefutsoth Photo Archive, courtesy of E. Nissim)

Mountain Jews, migrants from Dagestan to the Northern Caucasus, Northern Caucasus, 1930. (Russian Museum of Ethnography)

The Kuba women's costume (cat. nos 31–36, 38, 39) is similar to that worn by Azerbaijani women. The Miller collection contains an almost complete set, including a blouse, a jacket, a belt, socks and the complex headgear. The blouse is of a tunic type, with gussets and stitched sides, a round neck with a vertical cut in front; long straight sleeves comprise two parts. It is green in colour, with red trimmings and two buttons at the neck, and silver thread on the sleeves. Azerbaijani women from various areas, as well as Tat Moslems, wore similar blouses.[14] Under the blouse, a woman would wear breeches, or rather a skirt with the bottom part stitched together. This type of garment was common in Azerbaijan. The long, tunic-type blouse originated in Eastern Caucasia, while the trouser-skirt is a combination of Mountain, Iranian and Turkic traditions. A jacket was worn over the blouse. Miller mentions that the Jews gave it a Turkic name, *chepken*, which means a warm upper garment. The jacket has a waistline, tailored back and short flaps. It is padded and covered with blue machine-made silk, with a floral pattern and cut sleeves. This type of dress was also typical in neighbouring areas. The headgear comprises a *chukht* - a modified shawl with a long pouch for the hair, *kalagai*, the shawl proper and *chargat*, the top, band-like scarf. A *chukht* is a typical garment for a married woman of the area. Jewish Tat women did not shave their heads, but hid their hair in a *chukht*, leaving a fringe and curls on the sides. Anisimov reported that a woman's costume was distinguished by the absence of beads around the neck, a lock on the forehead and long curls at the temples.[15] *Kalagai* shawls, worn over the *chukht*, are no different from those worn by Moslem women; it was a popular silk with a yellow printed paisley motif. A light striped scarf, twisted and arranged above the forehead to secure the *kalagai* shawl, is not mentioned anywhere as part of the headgear of an Azerbaijani or Dagestani woman. Apparently, it is unique to the Jews of Kuba. A wide leather belt (cat. no. 31), decorated with coins arranged in three rows and a massive silver buckle was worn over the vest. Two half-buckles were ornamented with a darkened pattern and have small pointed umbos, the buckle itself is covered by a round plaque with an umbo and inlaid green and red glass on the perimeter. These belts were typical of Southern Dagestan and Northern Azerbaijan, some of the craftsmen who specialized in manufacturing these belts lived in and around Kuba.

It therefore seems fair to conclude that the garments worn by the Jewish women of Kuba resemble those of the local Moslems, apart from the band-like scarf and, perhaps, the fact that it was made of a purchased fabric - although this is more a typical feature of urban dress in general and not particularly indicative of any ethnic origin.

Mountain Jew with a dagger, Dagestan. Photo by D.I. Ermakov, 1878-1916. (Russian Museum of Ethnography)

No. 1735 collection contains a number of jewels and small articles of silver, copper, semi-precious stone and beads. These can be divided into two categories: dress ornaments (cat. nos 16-30, 37) and amulets (cat. nos 2-8). Because most combine both functions, a distinction can perhaps be made based on other features. The first group (cat. nos 22-24, 28-30) comprises silver ornaments which formed accessories to a woman's costume - which would indeed be incomplete without them. This group has no ethnic or religious peculiarities. It includes a tassel - an ornament for a *chukht*, a necklace with nine silver Iranian coins, a chain of coins with pendants and three hooks worn around the head to secure a light shawl, a braid pendant of coins and chains (clearly part of a set

Family of Mountain Jews at table, Caucasus, late 19th century.
(Beth Hatefutsot Photo Archive)

with the other ornaments), a breast ornament in the form of a rhomboid with open-work design and three coins. These ornaments were widespread in Dagestan and were worn both in combination and separately. They are always hard to date, for they often contain Russian, Iranian and Arabic coins. In the local culture a coin was regarded as a symbol of the sun, because of its shape. The group includes a round breast decoration - a silver fibula with inlaid coloured glass. It is called a *gul*, a rose, from the shape of the ornament, and was typically worn by Moslem women. Earrings with hollow beads and printed leaves suspended on chains, or a bracelet, linked by chains to four rings and a thimble were typical Moslem gifts to a bride.

The second group (cat. nos 25-27) combines ornaments that include cloth bags decorated with beads containing aromatic substances, and pendants with beads, shells and spices. This group includes a headpiece with a triangle pointing down (a universal female symbol) in the centre and two clusters of tassels on either side. It has the same name as the scarf (*yashmak*) with which the Moslem women veil the lower part of their faces. Apart from the *yashmak*, these items feature a pendant sewn onto the dress, consisting of a cloth triangle, six bags with aromatic substances and 43 clusters of vertically suspended beads, as well as a sewn bag, embroidered with beads and containing cloves. Spices were considered to provide magical protection, and were worn on the dress or kept inside the house: there were no particular differences in the ways they were used by Moslems and Jews.

Rabbi Yaacov Itzhaki, chief rabbi of Derbent, Caucasus, early 20th century.
(Beth Hatefutsoth Photo Archive)

Mountain Jews, migrants from Dagestan to the Northern Caucasus, Northern Caucasus, 1930.
(Russian Museum of Ethnography)

Family of Mountain Jews before leaving for Palestine, Derbent.
(Beth Hatefutsoth Photo Archive, courtesy of S. Manshirov, Israel)

The third group (cat. nos 16-21) consists of various items threaded together, erroneously referred to by Miller as necklaces, for these are smaller than the normal kind. Caucasians wore these on the wrist or attached them to a cradle, or a wall. Larger versions would also be used as necklaces. They contain a variety of items: amber beads, carnelian and other semi-precious stones, paste, stone, as well as buttons, kauri shells, rings, watch pinions etc. Some beads are clearly of ancient origin and featured in religious practice. All these pieces apparently represent the veneration of pierced items as symbols of fertility, purification or commitment - although they seldom bear any specific ethnic features.

Stones set in silver also served as amulets. Large pieces of jet (a variety of lignite, highly valued in the Caucasus), set in silver, were worn around the neck.[16] It is an amulet against evil spells called a *geikhal* (or *kheical*, according to Anisimov).[17] Among the amulets are brass and silver plaques with inscriptions. One of them, offering protection for women in labour and newborn babies, features a spell, calling on the 22- and 42-letter name for God, the name of Adam and Eve, the guardians of young mothers and the archangels. Other spells and protections include plaques which feature the magic quadrate. Similar amulets of carnelian, *serdolik*, silver and bronze came from Iran and Palestine.[18]

Besides the amulets with Hebrew inscriptions, Jewish religious items form a separate group within the collection. There are relatively few of these, but this is a major section of the Jewish religious collection. Among the items is a *mezuzah* case (cat. no. 1) with the first letter of the name *Shadai* on the front, a *shofar* (cat. no. 10) decorated with silver intarsia (locally called a *seyfer*), a wooden rattle used for Purim (cat. no. 9) (locally called a *jaryk*), Afghan *rimmonim* (cat. no. 14) two pointers for reading the Torah, chained together according to a local custom (called a *mil* or *milles*) (cat. no. 13), a Yom Kippur whip (cat. no. 15), a havdalah candle (cat. no. 12) made of 16 intertwined small candles, a pitcher for washing hands (cat. no. 11), a *hadas* of wax and cloves (cat. no. 48).

Young girl in a traditional costume of the Mountain Jews with breast pendant, Caucasus, *c.* 1900.
(Beth Hatefutsoth Photo Archive)

The *shofar* is decorated similarly to the typical Eastern Caucasian water vessels. Judging by the texture and glaze, the pitcher was made by Lezgin craftsmen, probably in Kuba.

Miller's Kuba collection is probably the most complete set of items relating to the culture of the Mountain Jews of Eastern Caucasia. In 1916 the St Petersburg museum acquired another collection (No. 3704) related to the Mountain Jews, this time from Derbent. By then Miller had shifted the focus of his research to West Transcaucasia, and had commissioned his student K.Z. Kavtoradze[19] to continue research in the East. Kavtoradze was assigned to collect items on Jewish culture in Derbent, thus continuing Miller's studies in Kuba. In the Middle Ages Derbent had been one of the major cities of the Orient and had had a Jewish *mahalla* (quarter, locally called *magal*).[20] The Derbent collection is smaller in size, it contains an ornate woman's costume, several religious items and amulets.

The woman's costume (cat. nos 49-58) suggests that Derbent's Jews were wealthier than those of Kuba. Judging from the literary sources and direct information, the Derbent community enjoyed a higher cultural and social status. All the components of the costume are made of expensive fabrics, covered with embroidery, including gold. The cut contrasts with the Kuba costume. The breeches are wider, trimmed with band, the tunic was shorter and both were visible. This feature brings it closer to the garments worn by Dagestani women. The tunic sleeves have gussets in the upper part. The dress is long, open, tailored with small gussets in the sides, and ample protrusions on the waistline. The opening is trimmed with a wide gold-embroidered band which, together with the red fabric, makes the dress quite spectacular. The sleeves are long and cut tighter at the ends. The headgear consists of a velvet *chukht*, decorated on the forehead with gilded paisley motifs. The *chukht* is covered with a silk scarf around the head, chin and shoulders. With a shawl on top, the ends hang loose at the sides. This was a typical costume for a wealthy Derbent woman. The costly Azerbaijani costume has certain features typical of Dagestan. Urban elegance is evident in the hooks designed as butterflies, and in the refined belt with open-worked heart-shaped plaques on the red background. To accompany the dress there is a necklace with a large silver medal featuring the tsarevitch, Alexander Alexandrovich, and Maria Fyodorovna of 1865.

A considerable section of the collection comprises items of gold embroidery. This was used for clothes, purses, headgear, certain interior decorations, small tobacco bags and suchlike. Wealthy Derbent women would have had plenty of time to devote to embroidery. It is difficult to say whether Jewish women indulged in embroidery themselves or purchased these articles. The detachable sleeves of a woman's vest (cat. no. 62), decorated with large discs made of spiralled thread were certainly purchased, since Caucasian girls generally made ample trimmings for their dress as part of their dowry and sold what was over. The spiral was a popular motif in Dagestan iconography.[21] A valance for the synagogue Ark (cat. no. 64) is embroidered with gold thread on brown velvet. It is made in a recurrent pattern of three-petalled flowers on long stems, with

Kuba woman's costume, front and back
(cat. nos 31-34, 36, 38)

Dress ornament, *gul*, Kuba
(cat. no. 28)

Kash amulet protecting mother and baby, Kuba
(cat. no. 3)

Yashmak, headpiece for the forehead and sides of the face, Kuba
(cat. no. 27)

String of beads used as amulet, Kuba
(cat. no. 16)

Torah pointers, Kuba
(cat. no. 13)

Rimmonim, Kuba
(cat. no. 14)

Ritual whip for Yom Kippur, Kuba
(cat. no. 15)

Pitcher for pouring water in synagogue, Kuba
(cat. no. 11)

Gold-embroidered valance for the synagogue Ark, Derbent
(cat. no. 64)

Khurjinn, linked shoulderbags, Derbent
(cat. no. 73)

Derbent woman's costume
(cat. nos 49-58)

additional flowers with triangular buds. These ornamental motifs are found in the gold embroidery tradition of Dagestan; placed together they make a totally unique design, typical of Jewish items in the Caucasus.

Two amulets in a remarkable five-pointed star shape (cat. nos 65-66) are also made with this gold embroidery technique. The use of a five-pointed star is common in Islam and is sometimes encountered in Jewish objects. Mountain Jews, from Nal'chik rather than Eastern Caucasia, connected the five points with the names of the archangels. Amulets were displayed on the walls inside the house.

The collection also includes tobacco bags (cat. no. 63) used as amulets which were common in Eastern Caucasia (specifically among the Azerbaijanis of Azerbaijan and Dagestan) and a signet ring with an inscription (cat. no. 60).

Two pieces listed as prayer mats and recorded as having been purchased from a Jewish household, are interesting, but also a little puzzling. Prayer mats are not used in the Jewish religion. Moreover, they are clearly Moslem prayer mats, so-called *namazlyks* (cat. no. 61). In Kavtoradze's inventory the angular motif in the upper part of the mat is designated by the Moslem term *mikhrab*. The mats are decorated with gold-embroidered circles marking the places to be touched by the head. The ornamentation is of combined stitches and the embroidery of multicoloured silk thread combines small and large floral patterns with a fringe. Similar articles are found in the museum's Kuba collection. Obviously, the collector did not record the real use of these pieces; they were probably thought to have been for interior decoration. Nevertheless, the fact that the owner of the pieces belonged to a different religion testifies to the religious tolerance of Derbent's Jews.

Miller's Kuba collection and Kavtoradze's Derbent collection date from a period of active research into the history of the Mountain Jews. It was to be 1991 before the next contribution was purchased from A.Y. Mikailov, the son of a Jewish carpet merchant from Krasnaya Sloboda, the Jewish district on the outskirts of Kuba. The carpets, decorated with various ornamental compositions, date from between 1901 and 1920 and had been stored after the revolution in the town of Gyandzha (Azerbaijan). They are accompanied by a variety of items, including a flat woven saltcellar (cat. no. 81) and a *khurjinn*. All the objects are connected to the Kuba area, where the role of the Tats in the carpet industry was more prominent than has until recently been supposed. Nevertheless, carpets from the other parts of Caucasia were also common in Jewish households. Anisimov, for instance, described Persian carpets in a synagogue.

Several items in the catalogue section were collected from the Tats of Dagestan and Azerbaijan and have a broader ethnic significance. They include socks with Tat motifs – providing an insight into the more commonplace clothes of both men and women – as well as various decorative items and carpets. Several pieces in the collection were acquired by Miller in 1909 in the villages near Kuba, and some items come from a mixed collection from Derbent, purchased from I.A. Ivanova in 1994. All these pieces are similar to those described in Anisimov's Jewish interior. They include a band decorating the upper shelf in the house (cat. no. 68), a strip of carpet with tassels for spoons (cat. no. 70), a Gladstone bag (*mafrash*) (cat. no. 72), a *khurjinn* decorated with eight-pointed stars (cat. no. 73), a pillow case (cat. no. 74) and a large carpet horse-blanket (cat. no. 67), made in *sumakh* style.

All these objects reveal the profound integration of the culture of the Mountain Jews in the world of Eastern Caucasia, although Judaism still dominated their spiritual life. Nevertheless, even their religious rites were ingrained with local beliefs. The alien cultures penetrated deep into the sphere of dress, house, food, while traditional Jewish prohibitions were respected. For the Jews of the Eastern Caucasus the synagogue was the central focus, but in the home they borrowed their neighbours' rites.

Jews lived in Eastern and Northern Caucasia, on the historical Silk Road and much of the area within the Persian sphere of influence, which remained strong in the eighteenth century. The unique position of the Mountain Jews in the world of Oriental Jewry is clear: their dual ethnic background and language set them apart from neighbouring Jewish communities; the men bore arms, there were traces of a special reverence to Jews who had converted to Islam, cultural borrowing was common in medieval times - as in the spread of Northeastern Caucasian etiquette and the introduction of the calendar.[22] The only credible explanation for this situation is that Jews had been living in the Eastern Caucasus since the earliest times, the period of ethnogenic population movements; in addition they may have had a role to play in the Khazar Kingdom's territory of Dagestan in the second half of the first millennium. Perhaps, indeed, it was from the Eastern Caucasian Jews that the Khazar Kaganate took Judaism as its official religion, remaining to contribute a major element to the early ethnogenetic formation of the indigenous people of Northern and Eastern Caucasia.[23] This would certainly have influenced the development of inter-ethnic relationships in the area.

Group of Mountain Jews at Khachmaz railway station, Northern Caucasus. Photo by D.I. Ermakov, 1878-1916. (Russian Museum of Ethnography)

While the Mountain Jews lived among the Moslems of Northern and Eastern Caucasia, other Jews lived among the Christians of Georgia and Armenia. The St Petersburg museum has a collection of objects relating to the Georgian Jews.

According to Georgian sources, the first Jews came to the area soon after the destruction of the First Temple (sixth century BCE). Later, Jews are noted around the time of the Roman Emperor Vespasian and in subsequent centuries with the Jewish language being mentioned as one of those spoken in Eastern Georgia. The conversion of Georgia to Christianity is associated with the activities of Judeo-Christian missionaries, the most famous being St Nina, represented in local lore as the patron saint of Georgia and protector of women.

Archaeological excavations near the city of Mtskheta (capital of Eastern Georgia until replaced by Tbilisi) have revealed Jewish monuments dating from the sixth century CE.[24] Later, the original migrants were joined by Jews from Iran.[25] Eastern and European travellers regularly mention the Jewish communities of medieval Georgia.[26] According to these sources, Jews formed a dependent class in feudal Georgia, including peasants, artisans and small-scale merchants. Jews were allowed to own small plots of land, some even became petty feudal lords. In the Middle Ages responsibilities of individual Jews were determined by social status rather than ethnic or religious background. This system collapsed in the chaotic period of dynastic warfare and the Persian and Turkish invasions.[27] Stability returned to Transcaucasia with the advance of the Russians, yet for the Georgian Jews Russian policies in the Caucasus led to a decline in traditional areas of employment. The abolition of serfdom in 1864 left Jews landless, while the Russian government raised restrictions on trade in various agricultural products. The second half of the nineteenth century saw the rise of urbanization in Georgia, which particularly affected the old Georgian cities. Rural Jewish communities shrank, while the Jewish population increased in Northern (Sukhumi, Poti, Batumi, Kutaisi) and Eastern (Tbilisi, Tskhinvali) Georgia.[28] Most Jews became petty artisans (cobblers, sweepers, shoe-polishers) or pedlars and petty traders. According to Pulner, in the mid-1920s most of the Jews of Kutaisi sold second-hand clothes in the villages, and bought fruit to sell in the city; there were 100 cigarette vendors and 10 porters. In Tskhinvali, according to the same source, 8-10 Jews out of 400 families worked as navvies.[29] The Jews of Georgia were engaged in quite different occupations: the Ashkenazim, immigrants from Russia, were artisans, watchmakers, jewellers; while the urban Jews who came from the Georgian countryside, were involved in leather processing. The difference was also evident in the language they spoke: the Georgian Jews spoke Georgian and the Ashkenazim spoke Yiddish.

Georgian Jews specialized in petty trading, travelling short distances, in the early twentieth century; large-scale trading was in the hands of the Armenians. The museum collection highlights the traditional culture of Jews in the towns of Akhaltsikh, Tbilisi and Tskhinvali. These centres reflect the pattern of Jewish settlement in Eastern Georgia: they are all located along the main Georgian highway, connecting Georgia with Northern Caucasia and Turkey. Western Georgia is represented by items from Kutaisi.

Market in Tbilisi.
Photo by D.I. Ermakov, 1878-1916.
(Russian Museum of Ethnography)

Jewish family in front of their house, Kulashi.
Photo by the documentation delegation of the Tbilisi Museum of the Georgian Jews, 1937.
(Ben-Zvi Institute, Jerusalem)

In 1903, the bridal costume of a woman from Akhaltsikh (now Akhaltsikhe) was purchased from M.I. Charukhiev, a well-known collector of valuable artifacts and weapons, by G.I. Gogol-Yanovsky on behalf of the Museum (cat. nos 110-119). The costume comprises a long silk blouse of a tunic-type cut, with a straight slit in front, two lined silk *kaptals*, a complex headgear, a necklace, earrings and footwear. The terms for the items are partly Georgian (for the blouse, the outer-*kaptal*, scarfs and footwear) and partly Turkic (under-*kaptal*, breast ornament). The tunic (*perangi*) is of a traditional Caucasian cut, the under-*kaptal* (*zibuni*) juts out at the side, like the dresses worn by Azerbaijani women, the outer-*kaptal* (*kaba*) also juts out, but less so. The headgear comprises two scarfs - one tied at the top and covering the lower part of the face, the other, darker, is twisted together and placed on top as a diadem. A similar arrangement is found in the Kuba costume, although most women in Georgia, and generally in the Caucasus, wore a different type of headgear. A white tulle veil, known in Georgian as a *lechaki* or *chikila* was worn loosely over the head. The footwear consists of yellow leather boots, embroidered with silk (in Georgian towns they would be made especially for a bride) and wooden *sabo* shoes, covered with leather, velvet and embroidery (universal in the Near East). The fabrics were manufactured in Turkey: they are too colourful to have been made in Georgia. The dome-like earrings with pendants are similar to those of Eastern Caucasia, yet have a Georgian name. The necklace of gilded metal is decorated with three medallions, the main part consisting of poinconnee fish-shaped links, typical of Transcaucasia, where a fish in female ornaments was an apotropaic symbol of fertility. In general, this costume is typical of Akhaltsikh, a multi-cultural city, principally involved in trade with Turkey.[30] The costume is registered at the museum as collection No. 258.

Next to arrive was a miscellaneous collection (No. 6397) obtained in 1939 from the Georgian Museum of Jewish History and Ethnography (cat. nos 120-137). This acquisition predates that museum's final phase, but was perhaps a signal of the museum's impending demise in 1951. The collection came to St Petersburg when the Jewish department closed. It includes men's and women's clothes, as well as secular and religious items. The women's garments come from Akhaltsikh, and form part of a sumptuous costume. They include striped loose women's breeches, a loose tunic-like blouse with large gussets in the lower section, similar to women's garments of other peoples. The outer-dresses, buttonless and open necked, combine woolen cloth embroidered in black thread and silk cloth with a woven floral pattern. Loose sleeves may have had lace on the inside. The bright colours are a general ethnic feature, while the inventory reveals these to have been either part of a bride's dress, a poor person's Sabbath clothes, or the everyday apparel of the rich.[31]

The men's garments form a disparate selection, the long striped silk gown worn by a *hakham* comes from Akhaltsikh (cat. no. 124); the overgarments differ from those worn by Caucasians not just in colour, but also because of their full length and the straight fastening up to the collar. Several overgarments known as *arkhalukh* (a short tunic, worn separately or under a longer garment) are from Tskhinvali (Northeast Georgia, later the centre of South Osetia). All these items were worn underneath a long *chokha*. One, made of silk, with a stand-up collar and buttoned front and small fine gussets on the flaps, is typical of the urban and West Georgian style, similar in fact to the general Caucasian pattern, although a note in the inventory states that it was worn by Jews of the mountain area, especially Tskhinvali. A striped silk sleeveless waistcoat with embroidered front would sometimes be worn under a *arkhalukh*. The collection also includes a long, colourful *arkhalukh*, with a semi-fastened slit at the neck. Clearly, anyone wearing this *arkhalukh*, would have stood out among the austerely dressed inhabitants of the Georgia-Osetian border country.

Other items in the collection include typical shawls and tablecloths of Eastern Georgia. Several household utensils and religious items arrived together with the garments. The household artifacts represent everyday objects: a clay kitchen pot, a turned wooden mortar, a snuff box, a water jug. These pieces have no specific ethnic features and would probably have been bought at the local market. A brass bowl (cat. no. 135) with a convex cross-pattern underneath is of some interest. This is a Caucasian bathing accessory, obviously older than the other pieces and probably passed down from one generation to the next as part of a dowry. The religious items are typically Jewish. There is a *shofar* (cat. no. 125), not decorated but carved at the wide end by a *hakham* in Tskhinvali. *Shofars* were kept both in the home and in synagogue. A tin synagogue collection box (cat. no. 137) is inscribed as being for purchasing flour for Passover mazzot for the poor. There is a *hadas* (cat. no. 130) for cloves and pepper for the havdalah ceremony.

In 1948 the collections of the former Moscow Museum of Ethnic Studies came to St Petersburg. This museum, which once owned a wealth of items, had been closed shortly before the Second World War, and in later years its collections were dispersed. Some of these pieces, hardly documented at all, were transferred to the St Petersburg museum. It seems that the bulk of the Georgian Jewish collection had been assembled in 1929-1930 by M. Plisetsky,[32] an authority on Jewish ethnography.

Wealthy woman's or bridal costume, Akhaltsikh (cat. nos 181–185)

Urban woman's costume, Akhaltsikh
(cat. nos 178–180)

Man's costume, Georgia
(cat. nos 123, 158, 159)

Rabbi's gown, Akhaltsikh
(cat. no. 124)

The Moscow collection augmented three categories at the St Petersburg museum: household utensils, costume and religious items, with a separate group of Georgian Jewish musical instruments. The household utensils include wooden, ceramic and brass objects. Among them are turned milk and water bowls, a scoop for flour, spoons, several ceramic vessels, including moulded, earthenware, glazed and polished objects, particularly the famous *shroshi* pieces from Western Georgia. Among the brass items are typical Georgian water vessels, *tungi*, and pots common throughout the Caucasus. There seems little doubt that all these pieces, with the possible exception of the spoons, were made by non-Jews.

Among the ceramics is a flat dish of hard clay inscribed in Yiddish, 'Bread, meat and fish are a joy at table' (cat. no. 174). Dishes of this sort were common in Europe,[33] although the clay and glaze are reminiscent of Tbilisi pottery, where the object may have been commissioned.

An interesting group of household utensils are the children's items: cradle linen, covers and amulets for children (cat. nos 163-170). The sheets were specifically for the type of rocking cradle common in the East; a baby would spend its first year in swaddling clothes, lying on its back in the cradle, tied down in a way that could sometimes cause deformity of the cervix. An amulet made of a strip of black cloth would be attached to the crib. For boys, the circumcised foreskin would be sewn into one of the strips. In Caucasian tradition, the detached foreskin provided protection, often being buried beneath the threshold of the house or thrown onto the roof beams.[34] Among Jews, the black of the cloth was also protective.

The other amulet is like an envelope of colourful triangular pieces of cloth sewn together, with a button in the centre. Mothers believed that it would protect sons against epilepsy. A satin amulet shaped like a tobacco pouch with a cover contains a scrap of paper with Arabic and Hebrew letters. This type of amulet would be attached to the child's back. Obviously, the piece of paper

Passover Seder at a Jewish home, Tbilisi, 1924.
(Beth Hatefutsoth Photo Archive, courtesy of L. Danielov, Holon)

Pupils of the Jewish school in front of the synagogue, Oni, Georgia, 1910. (Beth Hatefutsoth Photo Archive, courtesy of S. Hananshvili)

was a valuable object if it had letters on it, even if misspelled. Leather amulets containing pieces of paper include one with a picture of a baby in red ink, apparently drawn by a child, and some scribblings resembling Hebrew or Georgian letters. Any written text could serve as an amulet; the collection contains a piece of white cloth with encircled Arabic inscriptions and a female silhouette in a magic quadrate.

Besides children's keepsakes, the Moscow collections feature several amulets of a different type. One is a glass plate with a printed text (cat. no. 172) - featuring the name for God, the names of angels, inscriptions for the house and the word 'Jerusalem' in a *Magen David*. This amulet was brought from Palestine. Another (cat. no. 173), consisting of cardboard circles upholstered with colourful fabrics, has not so far been identified and its origin is therefore unknown. The collection also contains a copper Sabbath candlestick (cat. no. 138) and a parchment scroll of the Book of Esther, made in Palestine (cat. no. 151).

The musical instruments (cat. nos 152-157) acquired from the Moscow Museum include a group of stringed instruments - plucked and bowed - typical of Transcaucasia and the Near East. The group is completed with a drum. Caucasian Jewish music has been examined by I. Cherny.[35]

The Georgian Jewish garments from the Moscow Museum of Ethnic Studies are rather plain, the unique elements having been lost in the rise of urban fashions. Interesting items are woman's hairpieces with braid and side locks (cat. nos 160-161). The latter are clearly the hair of a married Jewish woman. In fact, Georgian women in general often wore artificial hair.[36] Since there is no apparent reason for this in Georgian culture, it seems clear that this was directly borrowed from Jewish culture.

The latest contribution to the Georgian Jewish collection (cat. nos 176-189) dates from 1974 and was purchased from a certain Mr Moshashvili. This collection (No. 8385) features garments from Akhaltsikh, dating from the late nineteenth century. Men's clothes are represented by a bathrobe with a customs stamp on the lower section (cat. no. 186). The robe was part of a dowry, or at least one of the gifts presented by the bride's family. It was brought by the bride's father from Turkey.

Women's garments are more amply represented. Various miscellaneous pieces include a Caucasian blouse, a dress of flower-patterned fabric with open neck and three sets of fasteners. There are also complete costumes, one consisting of a blouse and a skirt (cat. no. 178). The blouse has a waistline, a basque and folds on the shoulder; the skirt is finely plaited, with a hook on the left. These garments are unusual for the area, particularly Caucasia, betraying the European and Russian influences that spread to the urban areas. A local element has been preserved in the colour scheme of the clothes. The second costume (cat. nos 181-184), while not complete, is certainly more traditional. It includes a blouse and dress, striped silk breeches with a wide step, enlarged with an inserted gusset. A peculiar feature of this group is a fur-trimmed velvet coat with slit sleeves (cat. no. 184). These clothes would have been owned by women of wealthy or influential urban families, and were worn in the warmer months as status symbols. The collection features thick silk fabrics that formed part of everyday female headgear. Girls would wear these loosely over the head; married women would wear them over the two shawls with which they covered their hair. Embroidered towels provide a sample of urban needlecraft. A towel embroider-

Jewish women in traditional costume, Akhaltsikh, 1936.
(Beth Hatefutsoth Photo Archive)

Georgian Jewish merchant, photo taken in Odessa, 1910.
(Beth Hatefutsoth Photo Archive, courtesy G. Kurkuchshvili)

ed in gilt-thread, increasingly out of fashion in the early twentieth century, is an exceptional survival (cat. no. 189). This would have been used in the wedding ceremony – thrown over a cone of sugar to symbolize the joining of two families. Georgian gilt-thread embroidery was a speciality of Jewish women, whom non-Jewish Georgians often employed as embroidery tutors.37

One of the most interesting pieces in the collection is a square piece of cloth that the original owner referred to as *mizrah-supra* (cat. no. 188). A *mizrah* is placed in the room to show the direction of Jerusalem, *supra* is the Georgian word for tablecloth. It is curiously decorated. In the centre is a printed Hebrew text for the Sabbath with illustrations made in the printing house of Halevi Zukkerman in Jerusalem. The central section features an heraldic design flanked by lions with an inscription above a seven-branched Menorah and religious objects, with on either side pictures of the holy places in Palestine. Inscribed above is the text 'Remember the Sabbath to keep it holy'. The printed pattern is flanked on four sides by strips of coloured cloth, probably manufactured in Turkey. In general, it resembles local shawls that were used to cover fruit bowls, or *bokhcha* napkins used to wrap and carry small articles.

A major part of the St Petersburg collection of Georgian Jewish items comprises garments, mainly women's clothes, from Akhaltsikh. Clearly, Cherny was correct in stating that the clothes of Georgian Jews differed only slightly from those worn by other local people.38 The differences lie mainly in the

Carpet shop, Tbilisi. Photo by D.I. Ermakov, late 19th century. (Janashia Museum, Georgia)

Wool and carpet shop in the market, Tbilisi. Photo by D.I. Ermakov, late 19th century. (Janashia Museum, Georgia)

brighter colours, the predilection for larger, 'upholstery' patterns, the layered structure of the dress and headgear, more typical of Moslem than Christian Georgian fashions. This can be partly explained by the proximity of Turkey. Akhaltsikh's Jewish garments are referred to in various academic studies.[39]

This affinity with local culture is reflected in the household artifacts. The interrelation of the cultures is also found in the use of amulets that combine Jewish concepts with local religious customs. Another example of the similarity of these cultures is the types of ritual bread. A set of religious items indicates that the Sabbath and the annual festivals, as well as other rituals, were meticulously observed. A book (cat. no. 193), a manual for amulets and spells, written in various Hebrew scripts, testifies to the popularity of mysticism.

Another source of information on the culture of Caucasia's Jews is photography. Although small, the Caucasian Jewish photography collection at St Petersburg features several ethnic groups. In 1907 A.A. Miller photographed a derelict bath house in the Jewish quarter of Kuba with a group of women and children in front of the building and on the roof. The house is typically urban, with its flat roof providing an extra terrace above the dwelling. The women are wearing clothes similar to those featured in the collection. The absence of men and older children is due to their traditional aversion to photography.

Mountain and Georgian Jews are featured in the collection of the Tbilisi photographer and private photographer to the Persian Shah, D.I. Ermakov. The pictures date from 1878-1916 and feature men and women dressed in ethnic costumes, including a portrait of a Mountain Jew wearing a *chokha* and a dagger in his belt (see p. 80).

Relatively few items and photographs relating to the ethnography of the Caucasian Jews are known and little has been published. What remains provides a valuable glimpse into the culture of a unique and ancient ethnic people. Yet the lack of information about traditional Jewish domestic culture makes it difficult to form an accurate picture of the ethnic cultural balance of the Caucasus, the multilingual and multi-confessional bridge between Europe and Asia.

CIRCUMCISION SONG

Circumcision Song, recorded by ethnographer I. Pulner, Oni, Georgia, 1928. (Russian Museum of Ethnography Archives, Pulner Archive F.9, Inv. no.1, File 20, p.20) This is the first publication of an extract from Pulner's extensive manuscript (courtesy of RME).

Peace be within our walls and contentment in Israel.
Under an auspicious sign a son has come to us, may the Messiah come in his days.
May the boy be healthy, may he find shelter in the shadow of the Almighty;
May he study Torah, may he give the poor all they need;
May his ancestry be a blessing, his days long, his table prepared;
May his good name be preserved, let there be peace.
Come closer, friends, come brothers, to the circumcision, happy and joyous;
The Sabbath days are far off, there will be a time when they shall not be moved.
Peace be within our walls and contentment in Israel.
Under an auspicious sign a son has come to us, may the Messiah come in his days.

Mizrah-supra, Akhaltsikh
(cat. no. 188)

Boy's amulets, Akhaltsikh
(cat. nos 169, 170)

Crib set, Kutaisi
(cat. nos 163-167)
boy's amulet, Sakheri village
(cat. no. 168)
and crib, Caucasus
(cat. no. 84)

Notes

1. A student of Jewish folklore and ethnography, I. Pulner (1900-1941) became ethnography consultant at the Museum of the Jewish Historical and Ethnographic Society in 1929-1930; in the years 1930-1937 he rose to the position of chief librarian at Leningrad State Public Library, later heading the Jewish Department of the Museum of Ethnography in 1937-1941. As an Ethnography student at Leningrad University's Geography department Pulner conducted field research among the Georgian Jews. His findings are preserved by the Manuscript Fund of the Museum of Ethnography Archives.
2. I. Pulner Archive. Russian Museum of Ethnography (RME) Archives, F. 9, Inv. no. 1, File 1, 12: F. 9, Inv. no. 2, File 6, 7. (In Russian)
3. As an ethnographer and archaeologist A.A. Miller (1873-1934) researched Caucasian culture and was involved in theoretical and practical museum activities. In 1906 he joined the Alexander III Russian Museum's Department of Ethnography (EDRM), rising to curator in 1908 following his membership of the Imperial Archaeology Commission the previous year. Later, as director of the Russian Museum and department head he led the Northern Caucasus Research Expedition arranged by the Academy of Material Cultural History.
As a student of Eastern Caucasian ethnography, in 1907 he made his first visit to Krasnaya Sloboda in Kuba (Azerbaijan). In 1909 he studied the Jews of Kuba as a local ethnic group and collected household and religious items now kept at the RME.
4. J. Cherny, 'Mountain Jews', in: *Summary Information of Caucasian Highlanders* 3 (1870) p. 1-44. (In Russian)
5. I.S. Anisimov, *Caucasian Mountain Jews. Collected Data on Ethnography*, published by Dashkov Museum of Ethnography 3 (Moscow 1888) p. 171-322. (In Russian)
6. Vs.S. Miller, *Materials for Studies in Jewish-Tat Language* (St Petersburg 1892) p. 1-24. (In Russian)
7. B. Miller, 'Tats, Their Habitat and Dialects (Materials and Problems)', in: *Newsletter of Society for Exploring and Investigating Azerbaijan* 8/7 (Baku 1929). (In Russian)
8. M.E. Matatov, 'On Tat Ethnos', in: *Soviet Ethnography* 5 (1981) p. 109-111. (In Russian)
9. M.M. Khilov, 'Mountain Jews', in: *Peoples of Dagestan* (Moscow 1955) p. 226-240. (In Russian)
10. J. Cherny, *op. cit.*; Nemirovich-Danchenko, *Militant Israel. A Week with Dagestan Jews* (St Petersburg 1880). (In Russian)
11. 'Dag Chu Fut', in: *Caucasus Newspaper* 77 (1885); I.S. Anisimov, *op. cit.*, p. 190-207. (In Russian)
12. A.A. Miller's *Report* on 1909; Trip. RME Archives. F. 1, Inv. no. 1 File 49, p. 11. (In Russian)
13. E. Astvatsaturyan, *Caucasian Arms* (Moscow 1995) p. 37. (In Russian)
14. E.G. Torchinskaya, 'Traditional Female Clothes of Azerbaijan Peoples and Azerbaijanis from Dagestan, Based on State Museum of Ethnography of the Peoples of the USSR', in: *Ethnic Processes Reflected in Household Articles* (Leningrad 1984) p. 47-48. (In Russian)
15. I.S. Anisimov, *op. cit.*, p. 253.
16. We would like to express our gratitude to T.M. Gelfman, curator of the Museum of History of Religion in St Petersburg, for her invaluable help in defining the amulets of the Caucasian Jews.
17. I.S. Anisimov, *op. cit.*, p. 212.
18. I. Shachakh, *Jewish Tradition in Art. The Feuchtwanger Collection of Judaica*, Israel Museum (Jerusalem 1974) p. 306-312. (In English)
19. K.Z. Kavtoradze (b. 1879) worked as a freelance artist and sculptor at the Museum's Ethnography Department, and as a restorer and head of the Mannequin Workshop. Having worked at the Museum since 1912, in 1916 he was commissioned by A.A. Miller to do research in Derbent (Dagestan); the items of Jewish cultural interest he collected are now kept at the RME.
20. A. Istahri, 'Book of Ways and Kingdoms', in: *Collected Data on Tribes and Areas of the Caucasus* (1901) p. 88; A.A. Kudryavtsev, *Ancient Derbent* (Moscow 1982). (In Russian)
21. A. Golan, *Myth and Symbol* (Moscow 1993) p. 74. (In Russian)
22. J.V. Chesnov, 'Woman and Ethics of Life in Chechen Mentality', in: *Ethnographic Review* Vol. 5 (1994) p. 34-44. (In Russian)
23. A.V. Gadlo, *Ethnic History of the Northern Caucasus, 10-12th century* (St Petersburg 1994). (In Russian)
24. S. Caukhshishvili (ed.), *Kartlis Tskhovreba (Chronicles of Georgia)* Vol. 1 (Tbilisi 1955) p. 15-16, 36-38, 95-113. (In Georgian)
25. A. Gren, 'Transcaucasian Jews. Glimpse of History and Ethnography', in: *Ethnographic Review* Vol. XVI (Moscow 1893) p. 131. (In Russian)
26. Symposiums of Museum of History and Ethnography of Georgian Jews, I (1940); II (1943); III (1945). (In Georgian)
27. R. Arbel, L. Magal (eds.), *In the Land of Golden Fleece. The Jews of Georgia - History and Culture*, published by the Nahum Goldman Museum of Jewish Diaspora (Tel Aviv 1992) p. 45-50. (In Hebrew and English)
28. *Ibid.*, p. 51; A.S. Gren, *op. cit.*, p. 132.
29. RME Archives, F. 9, Inv. no. 1, File 1. p. 22.
30. L.P. Zagursky, 'Trip to Akhaltsikh Province', in: *Reviews of the Caucasian Department, Imperial Russian Geographic Society*, Op. VIII (Tbilisi 1873) p. 20, 31, 32. (In Russian)
31. RME Collection List 6397, Nos 19, 20.
32. A student of Jewish ethnography and folklore, Mark Plisetsky headed the Jewish Room at the Museum of Ethnic Studies (Museum of the Peoples of the USSR) in Moscow 1927-1940 where he compiled a collection of Jewish items. His collection of Georgian Jewish objects, gathered in 1929-1930, passed in 1948, together with other collections from the same museum to RME.
33. Sotheby's *Imp. Judaica. Ger.* (1989) p. 118. (In English)
34. R. Arbel, L. Magal (eds.), *op. cit.*, p. 110.
35. J. Cherny, *Book of Travels in the Land of Caucasus and Transcaucasia and Other Areas of Southern Russia* (St Petersburg 1884) p. 190. (In Hebrew). Cited in R. Arbel, L. Magal (eds.), *op. cit.*, p. 102.
36. Bocorishvili, G.A. Chachashvili, I.P. Brailashvili; 'The Georgians: Food and Clothes', in: *Peoples of the Caucasus* Vol. 2 (Moscow 1960) p. 301. (In Russian)
37. R. Arbel, L. Magal (eds.), *op. cit.*, p. 115.
38. J. Cherny (1884), *op. cit.*, p. 30, 136, 152; R. Arbel, L. Magal (eds.), *op. cit.*, p. 86.
39. R. Arbel, L. Magal (eds.), *op. cit.*, fig. 71.

CATALOGUE
Jews of the Caucasus
Mountain Jews

Mountain Jews represent the native Jewish population of the Eastern Caucasus. Traditionally, they lived in Northern Azerbaijan and Southern Dagestan. From this area they spread all over Northern Caucasia. Mountain Jews now live in Georgia, as well as in Russia outside the Caucasus and in Israel. The largest communities of Mountain Jews in Azerbaijan are in Baku, Kuba and Oguz (known as Vartashen until 1991); in Dagestan in Derbent, Makhachkala and Buynaksk (formerly Temir-Khan-Shura); and also in Nal'chik, the capital of Kabardino-Balkarskaya. Mountain Jews speak several dialects closely related to the Tat language, which pertains to the Western branch of the Iranian language group. In addition to being spoken by Mountain Jews, the Tat language is common among the Moslem Tats (who in fact call themselves the Tats) and the Christian or Armenian Tats (who belong to the Armenian Gregorian Church).

Statistics indicate that there were about 21,000 Mountain Jews in the late nineteenth century. In the 1970s their number was estimated at 50,000 to 70,000. The Soviet ethnic policy towards the Mountain Jews precludes greater accuracy. According to their records, most of the Tats (i.e. Moslems) resided in Azerbaijan and were thus registered in the census as Azerbaijani; Armenian Tats were registered as Armenians and Mountain Jews, as a rule, as Jews. In Dagestan (part of the Russian Federation), the majority of the Tat-speaking population consisted of Mountain Jews. Officially, all Tat speakers - irrespective of their religion - were regarded as belonging to the ethnic group of the Tats, one of several peoples of Dagestan. Mountain Jews frequently registered as Tats to avoid suffering ethnic discrimination as Jews. In the 1979 census over 20,000 Mountain Jews chose to register as Tats. Accordingly, statistics on the Mountain Jews are largely improvised.

For centuries Mountain Jews lived in the highlands and in the areas alongside the Caucasus close to the Caspian Sea. They believe they arrived in the area following the Assyrian exile of the Ten Tribes of Israel to the Median Mountains that they associate with the Caucasus. Aside from the legends about their origin, however, the roots of the Caucasian Jews date back centuries and remain largely a mystery.

The Eastern Caucasus is a strategic range on the map of Eurasia. This was the only route suitable for large armies (especially cavalry) to pass between Persia and Central Asia and Europe. All other routes were blocked by mountains and deserts. In the days of the Sassanids, Iran controlled these 'Gates to the Caucasus'; today the Fortress of Derbent, built under Khosrow Anushirvan, recalls this period. Around this time the Persian-speaking population (ancestors of the Tats) came to the mountains of the Eastern Caucasus. The Jews may have arrived at the same time.

Studies contain various theories as to the origins of the Mountain Jews. The ancestors of the Mountain Jews may have moved here from Iran and Byzantium. Alternatively, they may have come with the Arabic armies and adopted the local language of the Tats. Other sources submit that some local Tats converted to Judaism or, vice versa, that the ancestors of the present-day Tats were all Jewish, and that some adopted Islam at a later stage. Finally, the origins of the Mountain Jews are sometimes associated with the Khazar tribes. Between the sixth and tenth centuries Dagestan formed part of the Khazar Khanate, where some of the local population converted to Judaism in the eighth century. Unfortunately, all these theories remain highly speculative.

Nevertheless, the descent of the Mountain Jews from a branch of the Persian Jews is borne out by both linguistic and cultural relics. Mountain Jews have always maintained contact with Iran. Their communities expanded following waves of migration by Jews from Northwest Iran (the province of Gilan) until the seventeenth to nineteenth centuries. The Jewish quarter in the mountain village of Vartashen (Oguz), far away from the residential centres of the Mountain Jews, was founded during the migration from Gilan in the late seventeenth century.

Between the tenth and the eighteenth centuries travellers and geographers repeatedly reported a substantial Jewish population in the Eastern Caucasus, especially on the Caspian Plain near today's border between Azerbaijan and Dagestan between Derbent and Kuba. Jews also lived in the highland villages. According to most sources, they were mainly farmers and, occasionally, merchants. In the seventeenth century the Jews formed a large, thriving group in Eastern Caucasia. Several Jewish settlements existed in the vicinity of Derbent, in the valley called Juhut Kata (i.e. Jewish Valley). The centre of this valley was the village of Aba-Sava.

Many settlements of Mountain Jews were near old feudal centres. Krasnaya (formerly Jewish) Sloboda is a quarter of Kuba, Vartashen is close to Sheki, and Mudgi is in the area of Shemakha. Kuba, Sheki and Shemakha are former capitals of small Turkic kingdoms. The Jews sought protection from the local rulers (Khans), who welcomed them as taxpayers and as merchants. These relations, which arose in the seventeenth and eighteenth centuries resembled those between the feudal lords and the Jewish communities in medieval Europe.

In the 1730s, a fierce conflict broke out between Russia, Turkey and Persia in this area, ushering in a period of decline among the communities of Mountain Jews. In 1733 the entire population was massacred in the Jewish village of Kulgat near Kuba. In the 1730s and 1740s an army led by Commander Nadir, who later became Shah of Persia, pillaged Azerbaijan and Southern Dagestan. The troops totally destroyed the place and massacred the inhabitants. The oldest centres of the Mountain Jews, the cities of Shemakha and Derbent, were razed to the ground. In 1797 one of the feudal lords of Southern Dagestan, the Surhai-Khan of Kasi Kumukh, attacked Aba-Sava. After a fierce battle he occupied the village, annihilated all the men and deported all the women and children as prisoners.

Following these tragic events, Mountain Jews moved into

more protected settlements and founded the communities that still exist today. The refugees from Kulgat sought protection from the Khan of Kuba. They founded Krasnaya Sloboda across the Kudial-Chai River from Kuba, by then the capital of the powerful independent Kuba kingdom. Krasnaya Sloboda provided a haven for Jews fleeing the devastation caused by the Nadir-Shah in Central and Southern Azerbaijan. Jews from the highland villages and from the Persian province of Gilan started to settle in Kuba. The remaining Aba-Sava Jews moved to Derbent.

In the early nineteenth century the incorporation of Dagestan and Azerbaijan into Russia meant that the Mountain Jews became Russian subjects. In 1830 a thirty-year uprising against Russia headed first by Kasi Mullah and then by Shamil broke out in the highlands of Dagestan. The rebels founded a fundamentalist Islamic theocracy, an Imamate. All infidels (primarily Jews) had to adopt Islam or flee from the highland villages to areas controlled by the Russian army. The principal havens of refuge were Derbent in Southern Dagestan and Krasnaya Sloboda.

In the second half of the nineteenth century migration increased. Mountain Jews moved to centres they had never inhabited before, such as Baku, Temir-Khan-Shura and settlements founded by the Russian authorities, such as Petrovsk Port (now Makhachkala, the capital of Dagestan), Nal'chik (capital of Kabardino-Balkarskaya) and Groznyy, capital of Chechnya. Civil war stimulated further Jewish migration from the highland villages. They fled to the larger towns, such as Derbent, Makhachkala and Baku, to escape the Dagestan nationalists and the Turks. In 1918 a bloody pogrom broke out in the largest Jewish settlement of the time, Krasnaya Sloboda. In addition, the large Jewish community of Mudgi (over 1,000 people) disintegrated during the civil war, when almost all the Jews moved to Baku.

This migration of the Mountain Jews continued throughout the twentieth century. The fate of the Jewish community of Madzhalis (Southern Dagestan) is typical. Madzhalis is a vast mountain valley, containing three villages: one Dargin, one Kymyk and one once populated exclusively by Mountain Jews. Over 500 Jews lived in Madzhalis in 1886; in the 1930s a Jewish *kolkhoz* still existed there. In 1994, when the St Petersburg Jewish University expedition visited Madzhalis, only seven Jewish families remained. The rest had moved to different cities throughout Northern Caucasia in the postwar years. The Mountain Jews, once involved in agriculture, now live almost entirely in the cities.

In the 1970s migration to Israel accelerated this exodus by the Mountain Jews from their traditional surroundings. Although the Mountain Jews did not move to Israel with the same enthusiasm as the other Eastern Jewish communities of the Soviet Union, the growing political instability and declining economy in the Caucasus have made *aliyah* a widespread practice in recent years. War in Chechnya and the accompanying atrocities led in 1994-96 to an exodus of Jews from Groznyy and other towns to Israel, as well as to towns with Jewish communities in the Northern Caucasus.

Mountain Jews used mostly to be involved in agriculture, cultivating grain and grapes, fruit, vegetables, madder (*marena rubia*) - a root crop producing a red natural pigment, tobacco (in Vartashen and Mudgi) and fishing in the Caspian Sea. Landless Mountain Jews often did seasonal work in the neighbouring villages. Apart from agriculture, Mountain Jews engaged in trading, ranging from wealthy carpet merchants to pedlars. Leather processing was another traditional trade. In the early twentieth century aniline dyes replaced madder, leaving numerous Mountain Jews without an income and forcing them to move to towns to join the army of unskilled labourers, peddlers and the like.

When Russia captured the Caucasus, the situation of the Mountain Jews started to improve. The incorporation of the Caucasus into the Russian Empire probably rescued them from total decline and had the side effect of restoring contact with Jews elsewhere.

Mountain Jews differed little from the other Caucasian highlanders in appearance. Like their neighbours, they wore a dagger on their belts. This was primarily symbolic and placed the wearer in the complicated context of the clan, tribal and interpersonal network in which loyalty, tribal retribution and the like were regulated by *adat* (common law). Mountain Jews appear to have adopted all these Caucasian traditions. Ethnographers repeatedly noted the good relations between the Mountain Jews and the Moslem Highlanders, including symbolic acts of fraternity.

Mountain Jews have mixed Judaism with various beliefs of obviously pagan origin - common among the Caucasian peoples. There is an extensive folklore about natural spirits that control people's daily lives. Several homes of Mountain Jews contained symbolic items, such as a horseshoe, a stone with a hole, the so-called 'chicken god' and a specific type of thorn widely believed to possess magical powers among Eastern Caucasians. Mountain Jews eat this plant at the Pesah seder together with bitter herbs. They believe in the powers of amulets and use these extensively. In Vartashen a young Jewish woman, trained in medicine, acts as the local witch, protecting her customers from the evil eye. Her rituals include praying at holy sites also frequented by the local Azerbaijanis and Armenians.

Most Jewish holidays have different names among the Mountain Jews: Pesah is called *Nisonu*, Purim is *Gomonu*, Shavuot is *Asalta* (which refers to the sweets made by Mountain Jews for this festival), Hoshana Rabba is *Aravo* - which means willow in Hebrew; a willow, like the palm tree and myrtle, being part of the *lulav* used for celebrating Sukkot.

At *Aravo* the young girls gather for a night of singing, dancing and fortune-telling. According to accounts from Madzhalis, young men also take part in the festival by providing refreshments. Traditionally, all the supplies have to be looted. Looting is considered an act of bravery in Caucasian culture. The festival of the first of Nissan also has pagan roots. Young people go to the forest, pick flowers, gather dry wood and make bonfires and jump over them. This festival obviously resembles the Moslem *Kurban-Bairam*. Both celebrations contain traces of the pre-Moslem Zoroastrianism.

All the surviving Mountains Jews' synagogues date from the late nineteenth and early twentieth centuries. They are single-room structures. Derbent synagogue is decorated with landscape paintings. The other interiors are plainer, apart from the carpets on the floors. Mountain Jews have some characteristic utensils in their synagogues. For instance, the Torah scrolls are covered with two soft cloth cases; an inner one made of white canvas and an outer one made of decorative velvet. When reading the Torah, they trace the text with two pointers linked by a chain. Both the pointers (*kulmos*) and the *rimmonim* (of Persian origin) are made of generic, poor-quality silver by local non-Jewish artisans. *Kulmoses* are decorated with carnelians, corals and stained glass. Caucasian ornaments, including popular blackened silver, are used extensively. The ornamental style varies from one community to the next.

The Caucasus, especially Eastern Caucasia, abounds with ethnic and cultural diversity. Sometimes the villagers constitute a distinct ethnic group. Mountain Jews also live in polymorphous settlements. The following descriptions of two individual areas are based on my own findings.

KRASNAYA SLOBODA

Krasnaya Sloboda is a district on the banks of the Kudial-Chai river across from the city of Kuba. In fact, this area is unique in that its population consists almost exclusively of Mountain Jews.

Kuba has the advantage of being located along a busy trade route at the junction of the valley and the mountains in the centre of a highly fertile agricultural area. The Kuba kingdom's heyday was under the rule of Hussein-Ali-Khan and his son Fatali-Khan in the mid-eighteenth century. They ruled all of Northeastern Azerbaijan from Derbent to Lenkoran. The Kuba Khans established a Jewish settlement next to their capital, granting the Jews a plot of land and guaranteeing their safety.

The Jews that settled in Krasnaya Sloboda came from the surrounding highlands and valley villages of Kulgat, Kusary, Chipkend, Karchag, Shudukh and Kryz. In the 1780s Jews from the Persian province of Gilan moved to Sloboda. Newcomers from each area would found their own quarter (*mahalla*) in Sloboda and start their own synagogue. The section founded by Jews from Gilan (*Mahalla Gilyaki*) forms the centre of Sloboda. Today the people of Sloboda still remember where their families originally came from. The only active synagogue of Krasnaya Sloboda contains a large collection of some 70 *kulmoses* (pointers) from all the Sloboda synagogues. The number of shapes and styles matches the number of sections in Sloboda and the former number of the synagogues.

In the late nineteenth century the population of Krasnaya Sloboda stood at more than 7,000. Jews from Sloboda were constantly moving to other cities: most Mountain Jews in Baku are descended from Jews from Sloboda. Today there are *c.* 5,000 Jews in Sloboda.

The Kuba area is a world-famous centre for carpet making. Several merchant families from Sloboda dealt in the carpets produced by Highland Tats, distributing these worldwide, from Paris to Istanbul. The residents of Sloboda also sold textiles. Many peddled small items in the villages. Others were market gardeners who owned their own land, although they represented a minority of Mountain Jews. Most of Sloboda's poorer residents worked for the peasants in neighbouring villages. In the 1920s a *kolkhoz* was organized for the residents on land confiscated from former landlords, and a carpet workshop opened in Sloboda.

Even under the Soviet regime, Krasnaya Sloboda remained a trading town. Jews from Sloboda sold Azerbaijani fruit at the markets in Moscow. Today, commerce is thriving. Men from Krasnaya Sloboda transport Chinese goods through Kazakhstan to Moscow and other Russian cities, spending six months and longer away from home.

Trade has resulted in high living standards in present-day Krasnaya Sloboda, so that emigration to Israel is proceeding slowly, if at all. With a high birth rate, the population has hardly declined in the past three years (1994-1997). On the contrary, the Jewish population is gradually increasing. Families of Mountain Jews are moving to Krasnaya Sloboda from the neighbouring villages of Kusary, Khachmas, Khudat and even Baku.

Construction is in progress everywhere in the district as old houses are torn down to make way for new, luxury dwellings. The owners proudly exhibit both their wealth and their Jewish heritage: the walls and roofs are decorated with Stars of David, *menorahs* and similar emblems. The cemetery and the only active synagogue have been restored. Renovation of the largest of the surviving synagogues, the Kusar, is almost complete and will function as a community centre. Recently, a wedding hall decorated with Jewish symbols was built.

Unfortunately, the new houses are gradually replacing the old, picturesque Krasnaya Sloboda, built largely between 1890 and 1910 where the narrow streets with covered balconies recalled old Baku or Tbilisi.

Synagogue buildings dominate local architecture. Sloboda used to have eleven synagogues. Seven remain. They are all built of brick, the larger ones decorated with onion domes. The largest synagogue, in the Kusar quarter, has six domes. The synagogues resemble the mosques built in Kuba in the same period. Remarkably, the name of the architect of the synagogues has survived. Born locally, he was Hillel ben Haim. The houses he designed in Sloboda have also been preserved. The name and the patronym in huge Hebrew letters laid out in brick decorate each synagogue façade. This signature is virtually the only decoration on the sober synagogue buildings.

Unlike the people of Derbent, the residents of Krasnaya Sloboda show little ambition for their children's education. Boys become involved in commerce at an early age, girls marry even earlier. The newly-founded Sunday Hebrew school has not received much support. Significantly, the Jews of Derbent and Krasnaya Sloboda, separated by a small distance and only recently by a border, thoroughly despise each other. Derbent Jews consider their counterparts from Krasnaya Sloboda 'crude traders', while Jews in Sloboda view those in Derbent as 'smug' and 'good-for-nothing'.

Valery Dymshits

1. 1735-1
Mezuzah case
Elongated rectangular box with an embossed Hebrew letter shin, the first letter of the divine name *Shadai*.
Tin, 17 x 2 cm
Azerbaijan, Kuba, late 19th - early 20th century
From: Azerbaijan, Kuba, late 19th century - 1900s
Purchased in 1909 by A.A. Miller during an EDRM field trip to the Eastern Caucasus

2. 1735-3
Kash
Carved stone amulet set in silver, sewn onto a dress at the loop. At the front a Hebrew text with the 42-letter name for God and an abbreviation from the *Shemoneh-Esreh* prayer, with a square containing diagonal lines, the second charm protecting against fire.
Carnelian, silver, engraved, inlay, filigree, 3 x 2 cm
Iran, 19th century
From: Azerbaijan, Kuba, 19th century - 1900s
Purchased in 1909 by A.A. Miller during an EDRM field trip to the Eastern Caucasus

3. 1735-4
Kash
Square amulet with loops; Hebrew inscription contains names for God, the names of angels and a charm against Lilith, in the table below are ciphers representing the names for God. The amulet was worn by women as a protection for a mother and her baby against Lilith.
Silver, engraved, bronze loops, 6.5 x 6 cm
Iran, 19th century
From: Azerbaijan, Kuba, 19th century - 1900s
Purchased in 1909 by A.A. Miller during an EDRM field trip to the Eastern Caucasus

4. 1735-5
Kash
Rectangular amulet with loops, with the names of the five archangels and a charm 'In the name of Uriel'; below, the name of the woman who owned the amulet.
Bronze, engraved, loops 5.8 x 5.6 cm
Iran, 19th century
From: Azerbaijan, Kuba, 19th century - 1900s
Purchased in 1909 by A.A. Miller during an EDRM field trip to the Eastern Caucasus

5. 1735-6
Geikhal
Amulet with top-shaped stone set in serrated bezel with loops, sewn on a dress and worn on the chest.
Jet, silver, max. diam. 5.5 cm
Iran - Caucasus, 19th century
From: Azerbaijan, Kuba, 19th century - 1900s
Purchased in 1909 by A.A. Miller during an EDRM field trip to the Eastern Caucasus

6. 1735-7
Talysim
Spheroid pendant stone amulet with loops, Hebrew inscriptions on the edges and the reverse containing the 42-letter name for God and the name of the owner, Zelfa, sewn on a dress to protect against the evil eye.
Carnelian, silver, engraved, 5 x 2.8 cm
Iran - Caucasus, 19th century
From: Azerbaijan, Kuba, 19th century - 1900s
Purchased in 1909 by A.A. Miller during an EDRM field trip to the Eastern Caucasus

7. 1735-8
Talysim
Mounted oval stone amulet with dots and dashes around the sides, worn on the breast to protect against illness and misfortune.
Carnelian, silver, diam. 3.3 cm
Iran, 19th century
From: Azerbaijan, Kuba, 19th century - 1900s
Purchased in 1909 by A.A. Miller during an EDRM field trip to the Eastern Caucasus

8. 1735-10
Talysim
Round amulet with loops to form a pendant, featuring three moulded bead circles and inscribed in Hebrew with charms to protect against hallucinations, fever and the like, an anagram and names for God.
Silver, engraved, diam. 6.5 cm
Iran, 19th century
From: Azerbaijan, Kuba, 19th century - 1900s
Purchased in 1909 by A.A. Miller during an EDRM field trip to the Eastern Caucasus

9. 1735-15
Jaryk
Rattle for Purim, when the story of Esther is read and the name of Haman is drowned with noise.
Wood, carved, 59 x 37 cm
Azerbaijan, Kuba, 1880 - 1900s
From: Azerbaijan, Kuba, 1880 - 1900s
Purchased in 1909 by A.A. Miller during an EDRM field trip to the Eastern Caucasus

10. 1735-16
Shofar
Ram's horn decorated with silver inlay.
Horn, silver, inlay, length 45.5 cm, diam. 6 cm
Caucasus, second half of 19th century - 1900s
From: Azerbaijan, Kuba, second half of 19th century - 1900s
Purchased in 1909 by A.A. Miller during an EDRM field trip to the Eastern Caucasus

11. 1735-17
Pitcher
Long-necked glazed jar with spout, a single handle, a base and figures of birds; for pouring water in synagogue.
Glazed ceramic, moulding, height 36.5 cm, diam. 43 cm
Azerbaijan, Kuba and area, Lezgin ware, late 19th century
From: Azerbaijan, Kuba, late 19th century - 1900s
Purchased in 1909 by A.A. Miller during an EDRM field trip to the Eastern Caucasus

12. 1735-18a
Havdalah candle
Combination of 16 thin strands entwined.
Wax, cotton thread, 75 x 6.5 cm
Eastern Caucasus, early 20th century
From: Azerbaijan, Kuba, 1900s
Purchased in 1909 by A.A. Miller during an EDRM field trip to the Eastern Caucasus

13. 1735-19/1,2
Torah pointers
Two typical local pointers, flat with ornamental hand-shaped tops, linked by a chain inscribed with a Hebrew dedication and blessing.

Silver, carnelian, paste, filigree, chain, engraved, 26.5 cm
Caucasus, 19th century
From: Azerbaijan, Kuba, 19th century - 1900s
Purchased in 1909 by A.A. Miller during an EDRM field trip to the Eastern Caucasus

14. 1735-20/1,2
Rimmonim
Afghan type finials for a Torah scroll inscribed in Hebrew with a verse from Exodus 28:34, a dedication of Johanan and the 42-letter name for God.
Silver, engraved, stamped, 28 cm
Caucasus, 19th century
From: Azerbaijan, Kuba, 19th century - 1900s
Purchased in 1909 by A.A. Miller during an EDRM field trip to the Eastern Caucasus

15. 1735-21
Ritual whip
Twisted and braided whip with leather straps and wooden handle for Yom Kippur.
Wood, leather, 56 x 7 cm
Azerbaijan, Kuba, late 19th century
From: Azerbaijan, Kuba, late 19th century - 1900s
Purchased in 1909 by A.A. Miller during an EDRM field trip to the Eastern Caucasus

16. 1735-24
Necklace
Woman's string of beads of various origins, including a large stone and an amber pipe stem.
Amber, glass, stone (serpentine?), 44 cm
Eastern Caucasus, 19th century
From: Azerbaijan, Kuba, 19th century - 1900s
Purchased in 1909 by A.A. Miller during an EDRM field trip to the Eastern Caucasus

17. 1735-27
Necklace
Woman's string of beads of various origins, including archaeological pieces.
Glass, paste, 23 cm
Eastern Caucasus, 19th century
From: Azerbaijan, Kuba, 19th century - 1900s
Purchased in 1909 by A.A. Miller during an EDRM field trip to the Eastern Caucasus

18. 1735-28
String of beads
Supposedly a woman's necklace, the string of various beads include kauri shells and a metal pendant; some beads are archaeological pieces.
Glass, shell, metal, 18 cm
Eastern Caucasus, 19th century
From: Azerbaijan, Kuba, 19th century - 1900s
Purchased in 1909 by A.A. Miller during an EDRM field trip to the Eastern Caucasus

19. 1735-30
String of beads
Supposedly a woman's necklace, the string of various beads includes archaeological pieces.
Glass, stone, petrified wood, 19 cm
Eastern Caucasus, 19th century
From: Azerbaijan, Kuba, 19th century - 1900s
Purchased in 1909 by A.A. Miller during an EDRM field trip to the Eastern Caucasus

20. 1735-34
Bracelet
String of beads, rings, coins, shells worn by women.
Glass, shell, metal, 8.5 cm
Eastern Caucasus, 19th century
From: Azerbaijan, Kuba, 19th century - 1900s
Purchased in 1909 by A.A. Miller during an EDRM field trip to the Eastern Caucasus

21. 1735-35
Necklace
String of red glass disc-shaped beads, two pairs of jet and amber beads and nine Iranian coins with loops worn by women.
Glass, amber, jet, silver, 24 cm
Eastern Caucasus, 19th century
From: Azerbaijan, 19th century - 1900s
Purchased in 1909 by A.A. Miller during an EDRM field trip to the Eastern Caucasus

22. 1735-36
Head ornament
A chain with pendants and hooks worn by women as a clasp on a shawl and typical of Azerbaijan and Southern Dagestan.
Silver, carnelian, glass, chain, engraved, 42.2 cm
Azerbaijan, Southern Dagestan, late 19th century
From: Azerbaijan, Kuba, late 19th century - 1900s
Purchased in 1909 by A.A. Miller during an EDRM field trip to the Eastern Caucasus

23. 1735-37
Hairpiece ornament
Woman's chain with rows of coins, expanding downwards and typical of Azerbaijan and Southern Dagestan.
Silver, chain, 16.4 cm
Azerbaijan, Southern Dagestan, mid-19th century
From: Azerbaijan, Kuba, second half 19th century - 1900s
Purchased in 1909 by A.A. Miller during an EDRM field trip to the Eastern Caucasus

24. 1735-38
Brooch
Filigree quatrefoil in lozenge with coins hung from rings; a typical Eastern Caucasian woman's pendant sewn on the dress.
Silver, metal, 8.7 x 6.7 cm
Azerbaijan, Southern Dagestan, 19th century
From: Azerbaijan, Kuba, 19th century - 1900s
Purchased in 1909 by A.A. Miller during an EDRM field trip to the Eastern Caucasus

25. 1735-39
Pendant
Triangular pendant with six coloured spice bags and 43 strings of beads, sewn at the front of the garment or under the armpit; worn as an amulet by Jews and Moslems in the Eastern Caucasus.
Silk, cotton, wool, beads, glass, metal, 22 x 6.5 cm
Eastern Caucasus, late 19th century
From: Azerbaijan, Kuba, late 19th century - 1900s
Purchased in 1909 by A.A. Miller during an EDRM field trip to the Eastern Caucasus

26. 1735-40
Pendant
Bag containing clove and embroidered with beads, sewn on the clothes for protection.
Beads, clove, 4.5 x 3.5 cm
Eastern Caucasus, late 19th century

From: Azerbaijan, Kuba, late 19th century – 1900s
Purchased in 1909 by A.A. Miller during an EDRM field trip to the Eastern Caucasus

27. 1735-41
Headpiece
Band with triangular cloth, pairs of spice bags and lavish strings of beads to cover the forehead and sides of the face, resembling the veil covering all or part of the face of a Moslem woman.
Silk, silk thread, beads, shells, glass, clove, mastic, metal, 24 x 20 cm
Azerbaijan, late 19th century
From: Azerbaijan, Kuba, late 19th century – 1900s
Purchased in 1909 by A.A. Miller during an EDRM field trip to the Eastern Caucasus

28. 1735-43
Brooch
Rosette, *gul*, worn by women featuring numerous casts, inlaid with paste and coloured glass, typical of Azerbaijan.
Silver, paste, glass, stamped, filigree, moulding, inlaid paste and glass, diam. 8.5 cm
Azerbaijan, late 19th century
From: Azerbaijan, Kuba, late 19th century – 1900s
Purchased in 1909 by A.A. Miller during an EDRM field trip to the Eastern Caucasus

29. 1735-45
Bracelet with rings
Hinge bracelet with centrepiece attached to coins and chains leading to rings and a thimble for the middle finger; Dagestani workmanship.
Silver, semi-precious stones, metal, engraved, diam. bracelet 6 cm
Azerbaijan – Southern Dagestan, late 19th century
From: Azerbaijan, Kuba, late 19th century – 1900s
Purchased in 1909 by A.A. Miller during an EDRM field trip to the Eastern Caucasus

30. 1735-48/1,2
Earrings
Connected by chain, a pair of earrings with hollow beads, chains and leaf-shaped pendants, worn on the ears or in the hair.
Silver, stamped, diam. 4.5 cm
Azerbaijan, Southern Dagestan, late 19th century
From: Azerbaijan, Kuba, late 19th century – 1900s
Purchased in 1909 by A.A. Miller during an EDRM field trip to the Eastern Caucasus

31. 1735-51
Belt
Southern Dagestan woman's belt with three rows of high-denomination coins sewn on, two half-buckles with umbos and an inlaid disc.
Silver, leather, paste, stamped, chased, engraved, filigree, paste inlays, 79 cm
Northern Azerbaijan, Zakatali (?), late 19th century
From: Northern Azerbaijan, Kuba, late 19th century – 1900s
Purchased in 1909 by A.A. Miller during an EDRM field trip to the Eastern Caucasus

32. 1735-52
Chargat
A scarf worn by a woman, wound and tied around the top of the head over another (cat. no. 34), spread as a shawl.
Cotton, 213 x 22 cm
Azerbaijan, late 19th century
From: Azerbaijan, Kuba, late 19th century – 1900s
Purchased in 1909 by A.A. Miller during an EDRM field trip to the Eastern Caucasus

33. 1735-53
Tunic
Woman's garment with slits at the sides, open at the front with two buttons at the collar, straight sleeves and trimmed with ribbon and a fringe of silver-thread braid on the side slits.
Silk, cotton, silver, metal, length 105 cm, shoulder 46 cm, sleeve 60 cm
Azerbaijan, 1890s
From: Azerbaijan, Kuba, 1890 – 1900s
Purchased in 1909 by A.A. Miller during an EDRM field trip to the Eastern Caucasus

34. 1735-56
Kalagai
Rectangular shawl common in Azerbaijan, forming part of a woman's headgear, decorated with paisley motifs and extending past the waist.
Printed silk, 160 x 149 cm
Azerbaijan, 1880-1900
From: Azerbaijan, Kuba, 1880-1900
Purchased in 1909 by A.A. Miller during an EDRM field trip to the Eastern Caucasus

35. 1735-57
Shawl
Rectangular shawl worn by women, divided diagonally into red, yellow, blue, green triangles with tassels.
Home-dyed silk, 164 x 147 cm
Azerbaijan, late 19th century
From: Azerbaijan, Kuba, 1880-1900
Purchased in 1909 by A.A. Miller during an EDRM field trip to the Eastern Caucasus

36. 1735-59
Chukht
A married woman's shawl with a pouch into which the hair was placed, worn in the summer by Jewish women in Kuba according to the inventory and covered by a *kalagai*.
Brocade, silk, ribbon, metal thread, 107 x 28 cm
Azerbaijan, late 1880-1890
From: Azerbaijan, Kuba, 1880-1900
Purchased in 1909 by A.A. Miller during an EDRM field trip to the Eastern Caucasus

37. 1735-60
Pendant
Tassel with beads of various sizes worn by women with a *chukht*.
Ribbon, beads, glass, 70 cm
Azerbaijan, late 19th century
From: Azerbaijan, Kuba, late 19th century – 1900
Purchased in 1909 by A.A. Miller during an EDRM field trip to the Eastern Caucasus

38. 1735-61
Jacket
Typical buttonless open garment with tailored waist, gussets on the sides, short hip-length flaps, sleeves with slits and long cuffs, edges trimmed with ribbon, sleeves decorated with silver pendants, cotton lining worn by wealthy Azerbaijani women.
Brocade, silk, cotton wool, silver, length 60 cm, shoulders 44 cm, sleeves 69 cm
Azerbaijan, 1880-1890
From: Azerbaijan, Kuba, 1880-1900
Purchased in 1909 by A.A. Miller during an EDRM field trip to the Eastern Caucasus

39. 1735-62/1,2
Pair of socks
Typical woman's socks of Northern Azerbaijan - Southern Dagestan.
Wool, pattern knitting, 33 x 14.5 cm
Azerbaijan, Kuba, 1900s
From: Azerbaijan, Kuba, 1900s
Purchased in 1909 by A.A. Miller during an EDRM field trip to the Eastern Caucasus

40. 1735-63
Last
Arrow-shaped form for making knitted socks.
Carved wood, 30 x 11.5 cm
Azerbaijan, Kuba, 1890-1900s
From: Azerbaijan, Kuba, 1890-1900s
Purchased in 1909 by A.A. Miller during an EDRM field trip to the Eastern Caucasus

41. 1735-64
Spatula
Implement for browning grain and baking bread.
Carved wood, 68 x 8 cm
Azerbaijan, Kuba, 1900s
From: Azerbaijan, Kuba, 1900s
Purchased in 1909 by A.A. Miller during an EDRM field trip to the Eastern Caucasus

42. 1735-65
Rolling pin
Turned wood, length 72 cm, diam. 8 cm
Azerbaijan, Kuba, 1890-1910
From: Azerbaijan, Kuba, 1890-1910
Purchased in 1909 by A.A. Miller during an EDRM field trip to the Eastern Caucasus

43. 1735-67
Board
Implement for making flat breads and placing these on the oven walls.
Chipped and carved wood, 52 x 40 cm
Azerbaijan, Kuba, 1890-1910s
From: Azerbaijan, Kuba, 1890-1910s
Purchased in 1909 by A.A. Miller during an EDRM field trip to the Eastern Caucasus

44. 1735-68 ab
Spindle
Turned wood, length 29 cm, diam. 5 cm
Azerbaijan, Kuba, 1890-1910s
From: Azerbaijan, Kuba, 1890-1910s
Purchased in 1909 by A.A. Miller during an EDRM field trip to the Eastern Caucasus

45. 1735-73 abcd
Loom
Frame with thread, sample of cloth and slats to secure the threads.
Carved wood, 106 x 34 cm
Azerbaijan, Kuba, 1890-1910s
From: Azerbaijan, Kuba, 1890-1910s
Purchased in 1909 by A.A. Miller during an EDRM field trip to the Eastern Caucasus

46. 1735-75
Child's toboggan
Carved wood, 58 x 30 cm
Azerbaijan, Kuba, 1890-1900s
From: Azerbaijan, Kuba, 1890-1900s
Purchased in 1909 by A.A. Miller during an EDRM field trip to the Eastern Caucasus

47. 1735-76
Toy cradle
Model of a suspended (?) cradle with a crib set.
Wood, cotton cloth, 24 x 35 x 13 cm
Azerbaijan, Kuba, 1890-1910s
From: Azerbaijan, Kuba, 1890-1910s
Purchased in 1909 by A.A. Miller during an EDRM field trip to the Eastern Caucasus

48. 1735-78
Hadas
Wax pendant with cloves.
Wax, cloves, diam. 5 cm
Azerbaijan, Kuba, 1890-1900s
From: Azerbaijan, Kuba, 1890-1910s
Purchased in 1909 by A.A. Miller during an EDRM field trip to the Eastern Caucasus

Vladimir Dmitriev

Jewish women on the roof of a house, Kuba. Photo by A.A. Miller, 1907. (Russian Museum of Ethnography)

Derbent

Derbent is the capital of Southern Dagestan. The republic's second largest city is located on the Caspian sea on a narrow strip of land between the sea and the mountains and forms the famous Caucasus or Iron Gate. An ancient fortress is located on the hill. Two walls extend to the sea and surround the old city centre. The city itself is populated by Azerbaijanis, Lezghians, Armenians, Russians and Mountain Jews.

In 1806 Derbent was captured by Russia. Since a large Russian garrison was stationed there, the city provided a safe haven during the Caucasian war. Jews from nearby settlements in Southern Dagestan soon poured in. Between 1835 and 1897 the Jewish population increased from 472 to 2,190 and eventually accounted for about 15 percent of the population. Another wave of Jewish immigration from the highland villages came at the beginning of the Civil War. In the 1920s 7,000 Jews resided in Derbent, accounting for at least a third of the entire population. In the 1970s and 1980s about 15,000 Jews lived there (around a quarter of the city's residents). Many families still remember the villages where their ancestors were born.

Originally, the Mountain Jews of Derbent were mainly involved in madder cultivation, viticulture and wine-making, the fishing industry and trade. It was in Derbent that the first wealthy Mountain Jewish families appeared (the Dadashevs, who founded the largest fishing company in Dagestan).

Mountain Jews have never lived in a separate quarter in Derbent. They constitute around half the population of the lower, European town, while the Moslem population congregates in the medieval city adjacent to the fortress. This preference for the Russian part of the city is an indication of the cultural orientation of the Mountain Jewish community.

Even before the Revolution, Derbent had been the cultural centre of the Mountain Jews. Derbent rabbis from the Mizrahi family enjoyed a reputation as scholars. The chief rabbi of Derbent was recognized by the Russian authorities as the chief rabbi of Azerbaijan and Dagestan and as the state rabbi. The four synagogues in Derbent included an Ashkenazi one that served the European Jews who had settled there (and in other cities in the Caucasus) in the late nineteenth century. Today, there is only one active synagogue in Derbent.

In the 1930s the Mountain Jews started a theatre, as well as a folk culture group headed by Tanho Israilov and a Jewish newspaper published in Tat. A union of Jewish writers was even formed. Mountain Jews wrote their literature in the Derbent dialect of Judeo-Tat.

The Mountain Jews of Derbent - more than any other community of Mountain Jews - conform to the Ashkenazi stereotype in their quest for improvement through education. Many Derbent Jews are professionals: teachers, doctors, engineers. Since most were educated in Russia, they are fluent in Russian. Modern education has not, however, deprived the Jewish community of Derbent of its ethnic identity. A Hebrew school opened in Derbent in the *Perestroika* period. The main wave of emigration to Israel by Mountain Jews started in Derbent.

While the *aliyah* of the 1970s hardly touched the Jewish community of Derbent, in recent years, however, more Jews have emigrated from Derbent than from any other community of Mountain Jews. The high level of education among the local Jews is a major factor. Moreover, Dagestan is one of the poorest areas in Russia. Rising unemployment prevents skilled professionals from finding decent jobs. Dagestan's extremely high crime rate also stimulates emigration. Presently there are barely 5,000 Jews in Derbent.

Valery Dymshits

49-58.
Woman's costume
Eastern Caucasus - Dagestan, Derbent, 1900-1910s
From: Dagestan, Derbent, 1900-1910s
Purchased in 1916 by K.Z. Kavtoradze during an EDRM field trip to the Eastern Caucasus

49. 3704-1
Tunic
Typical Dagestani shirt with side gussets, open at the front and slits at the sides; straight sleeves, the slits and collar trimmed with galloon, the hem fringed with lace.
Brocade, silk, galloon, gold thread, gold lace, length 90 cm, shoulders 51 cm, sleeves 65 cm

50. 3704-2
Breeches
Typical Eastern Caucasian straight breeches with a wide gusset, lining and various fabrics, the legs trimmed with galloon and velvet, the lower section visible under the tunic.
Silk, cotton (chintz), velvet, galloon, 88 x 87 cm

51. 3704-3
Festive dress
Buttonless dress of a wealthy Eastern Caucasian townswoman, tailored back and front, tapered at the waist; open front trimmed with patterned galloon and lace, closed with three butterfly hooks at waist level with blue inserts; long narrow sleeves with appliqué patterns.
Brocade, gold thread, galloon, cotton, brass, paste, length 115 cm, shoulders 37.5 cm, sleeve 77 cm

52. 3704-4/1,2
Pair of socks
Urban workmanship.
Cotton thread, patterned knitting in the upper part, 24 x 12.5 x 16.5 cm

53. 3704-5/1,2
Footwear
Typical Caucasian footwear with soft sole and a seam along the sole.
Leather, 26 x 10.5 cm

54. 3704-6
Chukht
Shawl worn by married women in the Eastern Caucasus with a long pouch to hold the hair, trimmed in front with 20 *buth* paisley plaques and a central

plaque inlaid with turquoise, the lower end trimmed with a silk and galloon band and tassels.
Silk, galloon, gold, turquoise, stamped pendants, 93 x 26 cm, gold 35 grams

55. 3704-7
Belt
Urban variety of a traditional belt with a band of red Morocco cloth with openworked heart-shaped plaques, a two-part clasp with a lens-shaped buckle, trimmed with galloon.
Morocco leather, galloon, silver, chased, carved, engraved, 72 x 6 cm

56. 3704-8
Shawl
White woven cloth with pink stripes, a patterned woven fringe, *buth* paisley motifs and a label below indicating the 'factory of I.N. Vshivkin, silver 94'.
Manufactured silk, made in Central Russia for Oriental markets, 153 x 153 cm

57. 3704-9
Shawl
Woven cloth with oval medallion pattern, foliate motifs and rosettes.
Silk, fine weaving, 141 x 150 cm

58. 3704-10
Necklace
A string of cylindrical and spherical beads with pendant medal featuring a male and female profile and the inscription in Russian, 'In Honour of the Marriage of Tsarevitch Alexander and Maria Fyodorovna in 1865'.
Amber, cornelian, silver, 39 cm
Second half 19th century

59. 3704-12
Collar stud
Shaped as a leaf.
Silver, turquoise, diam. 2 cm
Dagestan, Derbent, 1890-1910s
From: Dagestan, Derbent, 1890-1910s
Purchased in 1916 by K.Z. Kavtoradze during an EDRM field trip to the Eastern Caucasus

60. 3704-14
Signet ring with cornelian
Hebrew text with the name 'Avraham' engraved on the cornelian.
Cornelian, silver, cast, engraved, diam. 2 cm, 3.5 grams
Iran, 19th century
From: Dagestan, Derbent, 19th century - 1910s
Purchased in 1916 by K.Z. Kavtoradze during an EDRM field trip to the Eastern Caucasus

61. 3704-16
Namazlyk
Originally a Moslem prayer mat, this rectangular ornamental carpet with a central oval cartouche of flowers, surrounded by a band of flowers, herring-bone stitching and garlands was used in a Jewish household as a floor or wall decoration.
Cotton, silk thread, satin stitch, chain stitch, 131.5 x 91 cm
Turkey, 19th century
From: Dagestan, Derbent, 1900-1910s
Purchased in 1916 by K.Z. Kavtoradze during an EDRM field trip to the Eastern Caucasus

62. 3704-19/ab
Detachable sleeves
Embroidered circles in a grid acquired separately as sleeve decorations from local Caucasian girls who often made a stock of golden embroideries as ornaments for dresses, purses etc. and which were often given as gifts or sold.
Silk, gold thread, 23.5 x 22 cm
Eastern Caucasus, late 19th century
From: Dagestan, Azerbaijan, late 19th century - 1910s
Purchased in 1916 by K.Z. Kavtoradze during an EDRM field trip to the Eastern Caucasus

63. 3704-21
Tobacco pouch
A bag with cord and embroidered ornamental mark for carrying small articles, money, tobacco.
Silk, satin, cotton, cord, chain stitch, 16 x 11.5 cm
Dagestan, Derbent, 1890-1910s
From: Dagestan, Derbent, 1890-1910s
Purchased in 1916 by K.Z. Kavtoradze during an EDRM field trip to the Eastern Caucasus

64. 3704-23
Parde
Valance for the synagogue Ark, fringed with tassels at the bottom and embroidered with a floral design on a long stem.
Velvet, cotton, gold thread, 56 x 43 cm
Dagestan, Derbent, 19th century
From: Dagestan, Derbent, 19th century - 1910s
Purchased in 1916 by K.Z. Kavtoradze during an EDRM field trip to the Eastern Caucasus

65. 3704-27
Amulet
Embroidered five-pointed star hung on the wall.
Cotton, gold thread, cloth, string, diam. 17 cm
Dagestan, 19th century
From: Dagestan, Derbent, 19th century - 1910s
Purchased in 1916 by K.Z. Kavtoradze during an EDRM field trip to the Eastern Caucasus

66. 3704-28
Amulet
Embroidered five-pointed star hung on the wall.
Cotton, gold thread, cloth, string, diam. 17 cm
Dagestan, 19th century
From: Dagestan, Derbent, 19th century - 1910s
Purchased in 1916 by K.Z. Kavtoradze during an EDRM field trip to the Eastern Caucasus

Additional items from the Russian Museum of Ethnography collection of Dagestan and Azerbaijan

67. 1328-8
Horse blanket
U-shaped cloth with a central pattern and magical animals and symbolic figures along the fringe.
Wool, pileless weave, 170 x 125 cm
Azerbaijan, Kuba area, 1890s
From: Azerbaijan, Kuba area, 1890-1900s
Purchased in 1908 by A.A. Miller during an EDRM field trip to the Eastern Caucasus

68. 1328-12
Ornament
A long band for a domestic pottery shelf, with fringed edge and embroidered foliate, zoomorphic and solar motifs and stringed beads.
Silk, silk thread, cotton thread, glass, paste, 227 x 21 cm
Azerbaijan, Kuba area, 1890s
From: Azerbaijan, Kuba area, 1890-1900s
Purchased in 1908 by A.A. Miller during an EDRM field trip to the Eastern Caucasus

69. 1328-16/1,2
Pair of socks
Patterned man's socks.
Wool, patterned embroidery, 33 x 15 cm
Azerbaijan, Kuba area, 1900s
From: Azerbaijan, Kuba area, 1900s
Purchased in 1908 by A.A. Miller during an EDRM field trip to the Eastern Caucasus

Items from collection No. 11644 come from a Mountain Jewish household in Derbent, where they were used for everyday purposes or kept as collectors items.

70. 11644-19
Spoon holder
An unfinished band of cloth with tassels for holding spoons.
Wool, flat weave, 59 x 22.5 cm
Dagestan, early 20th century
From: Dagestan, Derbent, 1st half 20th century
Purchased in 1994 in St Petersburg from a private owner

71. 11644-24
Printed design
Uncut strip of cloth with two designs for pillow cases, one featuring a peacock on a tree branch and the other a rosette with a foliate pattern and semi-circles in the corners.
Cotton, print, 103 x 54 cm
Dagestan, Derbent, early 20th century
From: Dagestan, Derbent, 1st half 20th century
Purchased in 1994 in St Petersburg from a private owner

72. 11644-26
Mafrasj
Square carpet bag for household utensils featuring a diagonal pattern on the front side.
Wool, carpet, flat weave, extra weft, 94.5 x 42 x 45.5 cm
Dagestan, Derbent, early 20th century
From: Dagestan, Derbent, 1st half 20th century
Purchased in 1994 in St Petersburg from a private owner

73. 11644-27
Khurjinn
Two linked shoulder bags, decorated on the front with diagonal stripes and spiral figurines in the central part and eight-pointed stars in the fringe.
Wool, carpet, flat weave, extra weft, 108 x 38 cm
Dagestan, Derbent, early 20th century
From: Dagestan, Derbent, 1st half 20th century
Purchased in 1994 in St Petersburg from a private owner

74. 11644-20
Pillow case
A bag with side openings, the front woven with flowers, a button fastener; stuffed with cotton or wool and placed on a sofa or on the floor for reclining.
Silk, sateen, mother-of-pearl, fine woven, hand sewn, 39 x 4 cm
Dagestan, Derbent, early 20th century
From: Dagestan, Derbent, 1st half 20th century
Purchased in 1994 in St Petersburg from a private owner

75. 1327-11
Rug
Rectangular carpet with fringe, the centre featuring an 'Eagle' composition and a zig-zag pattern.
Wool, kilim with holes, 185 x 379 cm
Azerbaijan, Kuba, Azerbaijani, early 20th century
Purchased in 1908 by A.A. Miller during an EDRM field trip to the Eastern Caucasus

76. 1328-1
Khaly
Rectangular fringed carpet with a central pattern on a red background, a floral and stellar motif along the fringe.
Wool, pile technique, 124 x 177 cm
Azerbaijan, Kuba area, Konakhkend village, Tat, 19th century
Purchased in 1908 by A.A. Miller during an EDRM field trip to the Eastern Caucasus

77. 1328-4
Khaly
Rectangular fringed carpet with six-pointed stars in the centre.
Wool, pile technique, 125 x 200 cm
Azerbaijan, Kuba area, Chichi village, Tat, 19th century
Purchased in 1908 by A.A. Miller during an EDRM field trip to the Eastern Caucasus

78. 1328-5
Khaly
Rectangular fringed carpet with central *golu chichi* pattern: a variation of *tapanchi*.
Wool, pile technique, 134 x 207 cm
Azerbaijan, Kuba area, Chichi village, Tat, 19th century
Purchased in 1908 by A.A. Miller during an EDRM field trip to the Eastern Caucasus

79. 11379-3
Khaly gebe
Rectangular fringed carpet with central *lechake torang* pattern from a Mountain Jewish family of Gyandzha.
Wool, pile technique, 103 x 190 cm
Azerbaijan, Gyandzha area, Chichi village, Tat, late 19th century
Purchased in 1991 in St Petersburg from a private owner

80. 4715-6
Namazlyk
Rectangular fringed prayer mat with vase pattern and large floral motifs in the centre.
Wool, pile technique, 134 x 205 cm
Iran, 19th century
From: Transcaucasia, 19th century
Transferred to the RME in the 1920s from Gatchina Palace

81. 11379-1
Salt cellar
Flat woven bag, decorated in front with motifs; used in the household of a Mountain Jewish carpet dealer.
Wool, 38 x 36 cm, neck 21 x 19 cm
Azerbaijan, Barda, early 20th century
From: Azerbaijan, Gyandzha, c. 1920
Purchased in 1994 in St Petersburg from a private owner

82.
Typical Caucasian man's costume, widespread among Mountain Jews
2nd quarter 20th century

a) 6085-2
Papakha
Flat top, with broad cap-band.
Fur, broadcloth, 13 cm, diam. 28 cm

b) 5915-3
Bashlyk
Hood.
Cotton, 121 x 58 cm

c) 6085-5
Shirt
Straight cut, open at the chest, vertical collar; sleeves with cuffs, the collar, opening and cuffs fastened with braid buttons.
Cotton, ribbon, length 95 cm, shoulders 50 cm, sleeve 65 cm

d) 11717-1/1,2
Cherkess chokha
Open upper garment, tailored front and back, gussets at the sides, straight sleeves and pockets sewn onto the chest containing *gazyrs* (bone or wooden sticks with jewelled tops, imitating cartridges) to form the most opulent part of the national costume.
Wool, cotton, ribbon, wood, German silver, length 120 cm, shoulders 48 cm, *gazyr* length 10 cm

e) 6085-10
Breeches
Tapered legs, narrow step, foot straps.
Broadcloth, cotton, sateen, 102 x 46 cm

f) 11723-2
Belt
Narrow leather belt with three side pendants, a clasp, a pointer, decorative plates and an imitation box.
Leather, metal, 181 x 1.5 cm

g) 8573-2/1,2
Boots
Made of front, back, top parts and with semi-soft sole.
Leather, 27 x 36 cm

83. 7293-30
Papakha
Man's conical headgear, with a lining.
Fur, cotton, height 25 cm, diam. 33 cm
Azerbaijan, Kazakh, early 20th century
Purchased in 1960 by E.G. Torchinskaya during a RME field trip

84. 8761-5342/a,b,c
Crib
A typical Caucasian and Near Eastern wooden cradle with a central hole and arched side walls, on curved runners together with a urine tube and a chamber pot.
Wood, 103 x 35 cm
Caucasus, 19th century
Transferred to the RME in 1948

85. 2956-81
Tripod
A support for a pot.
Iron, height 18 cm, diam. 19.2 cm
Caucasus, 19th century
Purchased in 1912 by N.S. Derzhavin during an EDRM field trip to the Caucasus

86-90.
Spoons
Purchased in 1916 by K.Z. Kavtoradze during an EDRM field trip to the Eastern Caucasus

86. 3705-126
Spoon
Wood, length 25 cm

87. 3705-127
Spoon
Wood, length 31 cm

88. 3705-128
Spoon
Wood, length 27 cm

89. 3705-131
Spoon
Wood, length 27.5 cm

90. 3705-133
Spoon
Wood, length 26 cm

91. 7103-89
Bowl
Spherical, ornamented.
Tin-plated copper, engraved, height 7 cm, diam. max. 16 cm
Azerbaijan, Lagich, early 20th century
From: Eastern Caucasus, 1st half 20th century
Purchased in 1958 by E.G. Torchinskaya during a RME field trip to Azerbaijan

92. 7103-92
Oil lamp
Shaped like a ewer, with horizontal spout and looped handle.
Tin-plated copper, engraved, height 23 cm, spout length 12 cm
Azerbaijan, Lagich, early 20th century
From: Eastern Caucasus, 1st half 20th century
Purchased in 1958 by E.G. Torchinskaya during a RME field trip to Azerbaijan

93. 7425-17
Cup
Decorated, with handle.
Tin-plated copper, engraved, height 11 cm, diam. bottom 14 cm
Dagestan, early 20th century
From: Eastern Caucasus, 1st half 20th century
Purchased in 1962 by N.P. Soboleva and A.L. Natanson during a field trip to Dagestan

94. 7705-11
Cup
Decorated, with handle.
Tin-plated copper, engraved, height 6.5 cm, diam. mouth 13.5 cm
From: Azerbaijan, Lagich, early 20th century
Purchased in 1969 by E.G. Torchinskaya during a RME field trip to Azerbaijan

95. 7913-33
Cup
Tin-plated copper, engraved, height 6.5 cm, diam. 13.5 cm
From: North Azerbaijan, early 20th century
Purchased in 1963

96. 8669-40
Cup
Decorated, with handle.
Tin-plated copper, engraved, height 10 cm, diam. 11.5 cm
From: Dagestan, Derbent, 1st half 20th century

Purchased in 1977 by E.G. Torchinskaya during a RME field trip to Dagestan

97. 10187-1
Pitcher
Typical Northern Caucasian vessel on a spherical base and ornamented.
Tin-plated copper, rivetted, height 60 cm, diam. 29 cm
Northern Dagestan, 20th century
From: Eastern Caucasus, 1st half 20th century
Donated to the RME in 1980

98. 10741-33
Milking pail
Tin-plated copper, height 27.5 cm, diam. 18.3 cm
From: Dagestan, early 20th century
Purchased in 1985 during a RME field trip to the Eastern Caucasus

The items in collection No. 11651 were made in the village of Lagich, Azerbaijan, in the early twentieth century and were used in the Eastern Caucasus in the first half of the twentieth century when first collected for the Georgian Society for Preservation of Monuments.
Purchased by the RME in 1994

99. 11651-7
Milking pail
Pot-shaped, with two handles.
Tin-plated copper, height 26.5 cm, diam. 19 cm

100. 11651-12
Milking pail
Pot-shaped, with handle.
Tin-plated copper, height 23.5 cm, diam. 21 cm

101. 11651-23
Bowl
Spherical.
Tin-plated copper, height 12.5 cm, diam. 25 cm

102. 11651-45
Tray
Tin-plated copper, engraved, height 3 cm, diam. 57.5 cm

103. 11651-48
Tray
Tin-plated copper, engraved, height 4 cm, diam. 48.5 cm

104. 11651-26
Pot with lid
Tin-plated copper, height 23 cm, diam. 24.5 cm

Collection No. 11677 contains items made in Derbent, Dagestan, in the early twentieth century and used in a Mountain Jewish household in Derbent.
Purchased in 1995 in St Petersburg from a private owner

105. 11677-2
Colander
Spherical.
Tin-plated copper, punched, height 12 cm, diam. 39 cm

106. 11677-5
Skimmer
Tin-plated copper, chased, length 50 cm, diam. 13 cm

The items in collection No. 11726 were made in Western Georgia in the early twentieth century, and were in use there when first collected for the Georgian Society for Preservation of Monuments.
Purchased by the RME in 1994

107. 11726-2
Frying pan
Flat bowl with handle.
Tin-plated copper, rivetted, chased, length 44.5 cm, diam. 23.5 cm

108. 11726-3
Frying pan
Flat bowl with handle.
Bronze, soldered, rivetted, chased, length 29.5 cm, diam. 14 cm

109. IB/01-141.IK
Map of Central Asia
Compiled by the Russian General Staff in 1869-1870.
Scale: 1:100
Purchased in 1909 by A.A. Miller during an EDRM field trip to the Eastern Caucasus

Vladimir Dmitriev

Jews of the Caucasus
Georgian Jews

INTRODUCTION

Georgian Jews live scattered throughout Georgia and outside, in Russia, Azerbaijan (with a small Georgian Jewish community in Baku), the United States and Israel, where their numbers are largest. In the early twentieth century around 30,000 Jews lived in Georgia. By 1970 the figure was 43,000 and in 1979, after massive *aliyah*, only 10,000. Today there are no more than two or three thousand. Jewish communities survive in Western Georgia in Kutaisi, in Northern Georgia in Oni, in Central Georgia in Tbilisi, Gori, Surami and Kareli and in Akhaltsikh in Southern Georgia. The once numerous communities of Kulashi and Vani in Western Georgia have ceased to exist, like the communities of Sukhumi, Abkhasia, and Tskhinvali in Southern Osetia. This seems largely to have resulted from local wars.

Georgian Jews are more integrated into the culture of their surroundings than their counterparts in any other community. They speak Georgian, each community using the local dialect. In the period of emancipation, the linguistic pattern of the Georgian Jews was unique among Jewish communities in the Diaspora. While the Ashkenazim and the Bukharan and Mountain Jews adopted or tried to adopt Russian - the language of the Empire - rather than the languages of the surrounding peoples, the Georgian Jews, traditionally close to the ancient and highly developed Georgian culture, retained their Georgian orientation. Georgian Jewish intellectuals have participated actively in Georgian culture.

Remarkably, Georgian Gentiles and Jews both boast that

anti-Semitism has never existed in Georgia, although historical facts attest to the contrary. Nevertheless, the misconception is interesting and reflects the role that Jews have played in Georgian national mythology. Jews settled in Georgia, on the periphery of the Near East, many centuries ago. According to legend, the Jews came to Georgia after the destruction of the First Temple. The refugees are supposed to have included descendants of King David, from whom the Bagratids, a dynasty of Georgian and Armenian kings, claim descent. Which is why the 2,600 years of Jewish settlement in Georgia will be celebrated as a national holiday, with President Shevardnadze heading the anniversary committee. The second important page in the nation's legendary history, the conversion of Georgia, also has a Jewish connection. According to tradition, the Jews of Mtskheta, the ancient capital, were present at Jesus' trial and tried in vain to acquit him. One of them, Elioz, brought a holy relic, Christ's cloak, to Mtskheta. His sister Sidonia touched the cloak, heard about the Crucifixion, died and was buried with the cloak in her hands. The main Georgian Orthodox cathedral, a masterpiece of Georgian mediaeval architecture, Svetitskhoveli (Pillar of Life) was later built on the spot where she is supposed to have been buried. St Nina came to Georgia in the early fourth century in search of the holy relic. The hagiography of St Nina, who converted Georgia, mentions that she preached to the Jews and so won her first souls. It has been suggested that Georgia is the Land of Iperic (or Iberia) mentioned in the Talmud. However, the earliest tangible evidence of Jewish settlement in Georgia is the sixth-century Jewish cemetery in Mtskheta, the country's ancient capital.

Throughout the Middle Ages Georgia remained the arena of continuous fighting against Mongols, Turks, Persians and the Highlanders of the Northern Caucasus. The local population, including the Jews, sought protection from the Georgian king, the monasteries or the feudal lords, thereby accepting serfdom. Georgia seems to be the only country where Jews belonged to a class of slaves.

The main occupations of Georgian Jews were agriculture and peddling. The Jews of Akhaltsikhe were also involved in cross-border trade with Turkey. Although by the end of the nineteenth century some Georgian Jews were wealthy, the Armenians dominated Georgian commerce.

After the abolition of serfdom in 1864, Georgian Jews started to move to the cities where they formed communities. In most of the Georgian cities the Jews were a minority, yet in some, such as Oni, Kulashi and Vani, they soon represented more than half of the population. The late nineteenth-century origins of today's communities, as related by the Georgian Jews themselves, is confirmed by the age of the first synagogues and the tombstones that date back to the 1860s and 1870s. Georgia's synagogues have no specific features; they are typical late nineteenth-century Ashkenazi synagogues, designed by European architects. In the centre of the actual synagogue hall, almost square in shape, is the *tevah* from which the Torah is read. At the western wall there is a cupboard for the Torah scrolls, usually called the *Aron ha-kodesh*. While it is indeed a cupboard, like the Ashkenazi *Aron ha-kodesh*, it has several shelves, resembling the *Hekhal* of the Eastern communities. The *tevah*, as in European synagogues, is often found under the inner canopy or between the four pillars supporting the ceiling. As a rule, Georgian synagogues do not feature outside domes, apart from the synagogue in Oni, based on a design brought from Poland, with its typical Polish dome. All the Georgian synagogues have women's galleries.

The synagogue at Akhaltsikhe is different from the other Georgian synagogues. For three centuries Akhaltsikhe had remained Turkish, and the local Jews become oriented towards Sephardi Judaism, although their language, family names and traditions reveal them to be Georgian Jews. Nevertheless, the graves of Akhaltsikhe's Jews resemble those of Jewish cemeteries in Turkey, and in the epitaphs the name of the deceased is preceded by the characteristic title Señor, obviously borrowed from the 'real' Sephardim. The synagogue of Akhaltsikhe is more Sephardi in style than Ashkenazi. The hall is elongated, with *tevah* and *Hekhal* (the terms used in Akhaltsikhe) located at opposite ends.

In general, Torah scroll repositories in Georgian synagogues are of the Persian type, although somewhat modified. Torah scrolls are kept in massive wooden cases, cylindrical or polygonal in shape, sometimes topped with a small wooden *keter Torah*. The repositories are covered with cloths. Georgian Jews employ various types of *rimmonim*, the most common being the image of a hexagonal pavilion with a dome. The Georgian name for a *rimon* is *tadgi*, which means both 'crown' and 'dome'. These *rimmonim* appear to be stylized images of the Mosque of Omar in Jerusalem, the Dome of Rock. Clearly, the widespread mediaeval Temple iconography in which the Mosque of Omar was equated with the Temple of Solomon had gained influence among the Georgian Jews.

The principal studies on Georgia's Jews are by Josef Cherny (see above). In 1934-1948 the State Museum of History and Ethnography of Georgian Jews opened in Tbilisi. The exhibits included paintings by the primitivist Shalom Koboshvili featuring the life of the Akhaltsikhe Jews. The Museum also arranged academic symposia. In 1948 the Museum was closed and Director Aron Kriheli arrested. The collection of the Jewish Museum was distributed among other museums and archives, primarily to the Georgian Museum. Hopefully, all these items will be exhibited in the now re-opened Jewish Museum. Recently, studies on Georgian Jews resumed with *In the Land of the Golden Fleece*, an exhibition in Tel Aviv's Beth Hatefutsoth Museum and the publication of an extensive book with illustrations.

Valery Dymshits

110-119.
Bridal costume
Garments of a wealthy Akhaltsikh bride.
From: Georgia, Akhaltsikh, 1900s
Purchased by G.I. Gogol-Yanovsky for the EDRM from the collector M.I. Charukhiev of Tiflis in 1903

110. 258-1
Under tunic
Open down to the waist at the front, this typical Caucasian garment has large gussets in the sides, straight sleeves, and collar and edges trimmed with galloon.
Silk, galloon, length 130 cm, shoulder 54 cm, sleeve 53 cm
Georgia, Akhaltsikh, 1890-1900s

111. 258-2
Under *kaptal*
Open at the front, the edges trimmed with braid; straight back and front, with gussets at the sides to enlarge the form; open lower sleeves trimmed with braid and lace and a spherical button at the hem. Turkish fabric.
Silk, cotton, silk thread, metal, length 118 cm, shoulder 40 cm, sleeve 66 cm
Georgia, Akhaltsikh, 1890-1900s

112. 258-3
Outer *kaptal*
Dress, open at the front, expanded at the sides with gussets, the open lower sleeves trimmed with braid and lace. Turkish fabric.
Brocade, silk, silk thread, length 133 cm, shoulder 44 cm, sleeve 65 cm
Georgia, Akhaltsikh, 1890-1900s

113. 258-4
Scarf
Triangular cloth wound and worn as a headband. Turkish fabric.
Silk, print, 137 x 51 cm
Turkey, 1890-1900s

114. 258-5
Scarf
Square cloth with paisley motif surrounded by a margin with a meandering line, wound and arranged around the face, the ends tied together at the back of the neck.
Silk, print, 90 x 85 cm
Georgia, Akhaltsikh, 1890-1900s

115. 258-6
Veil
Large triangular scarf with woven floral pattern, worn with the ends hanging loose.
Tulle, 270 x 210 cm
Georgia, Akhaltsikh, 1890-1900s

116. 258-7
Necklace
Row of fish-shaped links, with pendants, including hands, paisley motifs and rhomboids, with a central quatrefoil, all generally symbolising fertility in the Caucasus.
Gilt brass, punched, engraved, 37 x 13 cm
Georgia, Akhaltsikh, 1890-1900s

117. 258-8/ab
Earrings
Domes with pendants terminating in spheres, surmounted by rosettes leading to the hook.
Silver, filigree, grain, faux grain, punched, engraved, spirals, beads, 6.5 cm, weight 11 grams
Georgia, Akhaltsikh, 1880-1900s

118. 258-9/ab
Pair of boots
Soft sole, ankle-length uppers, embroidered with silk thread. Worn inside mules.
Leather, silk, 25 x 22 cm
Georgia, Akhaltsikh, 1900s

119. 258-10/ab
Pair of mules
Sabo shoes with pointed curved toes, open back, embroidered uppers featuring a flower with buds; heels studded with three nails.
Wood, leather, velvet, galloon, silk thread, cotton thread, iron, 24 x 7.5 cm
Georgia, Akhaltsikh, 1900s

120. 6397-5
Woman's breeches
Wide legs; part of a festive costume made of narrow-stripe cloth.
Silk, cotton thread, inside seam 85 cm, waist 75 cm
Georgia, Akhaltsikh, 1900-1920s
From: Georgia, Akhaltsikh, 1900-1920s
Transferred to the RME in 1939 from the Georgian Museum of Jewish History and Ethnography

121. 6397-8
Man's *arkhalukh*
Festive knee-length tunic worn under the *chokha*. Lined, tailored front and back with gussets at the sides, finely pleated waist and narrow gussets at the flaps. Small slit along straight sleeves; open chest and pockets at the sides below the waist. Pockets and sleeves trimmed with galloon.
Silk, cotton, galloon, gold thread, length 101 cm, shoulder 33 cm, sleeve 72 cm
Georgia, Tskhinvali, 1900-1920s
From: Georgia, Tskhinvali, 1900-1920s
Transferred to the RME in 1939 from the Georgian Museum of Jewish History and Ethnography

122. 6397-10
Man's waistcoat
Open sleeveless garment worn under the *arkhalukh*, made of striped cloth and lined. Embroidered at the front and with a pocket on the chest.
Silk, cotton, silk thread, 52 x 45 cm
Georgia, Tskhinvali, 1900-1920s
From: Georgia, Tskhinvali, 1900-1920s
Transferred to the RME in 1939 from the Georgian Museum of Jewish History and Ethnography

123. 6397-11
Man's *arkhalukh*
Caucasian tunic with stand-up collar commonly worn under the *chokha*. Open and embroidered chest, tapered back, fine typically Transcaucasian pleats on the waist, narrow gussets on the slit below and tapered sleeves. Collar, slit and sleeves trimmed with galloon.
Silk, cotton, silk and cotton thread, length 75 cm, shoulder 48 cm, waist 31 cm, sleeve 55 cm
Georgia, Tskhinvali, 1900-1920s
From: Georgia, Tskhinvali, 1900-1920s
Transferred to the RME in 1939 from the Georgian Museum of Jewish History and Ethnography

124. 6397-12
Rabbi's gown
Long open garment with stand-up collar featuring three string buttons, straight back, gussets at the sides, wide oblique gussets at the flaps and 2-button fastener at the waist; two slits for pockets in the sides and one on the chest. Cord with three loops on the left. Sleeves with slits and cuffs, trimmed with braid and plaited buttons. Striped Turkish fabric.
Silk, cotton thread, length 138 cm,

shoulder 49 cm, sleeve 72 cm
From: Georgia, Akhaltsikh, 1900-1920s
Transferred to the RME in 1939 from the Georgian Museum of Jewish History and Ethnography

125. 6397-13
Shofar
Rams' horn carved at the bell.
Horn, 22 x 6 cm
Georgia, 1900-1920s
From: Georgia, 1900-1920s
Transferred to the RME in 1939 from the Georgian Museum of Jewish History and Ethnography

126. 6397-14
Pot
Flat-bottom vessel with curved edge and diagonal lines on the shoulders.
Earthenware, black lacquer, height 12 cm, diam. 12 cm
East Georgia, 1900-1920s
From: Georgia, Tskhinvali, 1900-1920s
Transferred to the RME in 1939 from the Georgian Museum of Jewish History and Ethnography

127. 6397-15
Water jug
Extended neck with bands.
Earthenware, brown glaze, height 27.5 cm, diam. 12 cm
Georgia, Tbilisi (Tiflis), 1890-1910s
From: Georgia, 1890-1920s
Transferred to the RME in 1939 from the Georgian Museum of Jewish History and Ethnography

128. 6397-16
Spinning top
Turned with a whip.
Wood, height 8 cm, diam. 6 cm
Georgia, Tskhinvali region, 1900-1920s
From: Georgia, Tskhinvali region, 1900-1920s
Transferred to the RME in 1939 from the Georgian Museum of Jewish History and Ethnography

129. 6397-17
Mortar
Cylinder, with a central grip.
Turned wood, height 21 cm, diam. 17 cm
Western Georgia, Kutaisi (?), 1900-1920s
From: Western Georgia, Oni, 1900-1920s
Transferred to the RME in 1939 from the Georgian Museum of Jewish History and Ethnography

130. 6397-18
Spice box
Perforated cylindrical box or *hadas* for Havdalah.
Tin, height 6 cm, diam. 4.5 cm
Georgia, late 19th - early 20th century
From: Georgia, late 19th - early 20th century
Transferred to the RME in 1939 from the Georgian Museum of Jewish History and Ethnography

131. 6397-19
Woman's outer dress
Open garment with low-cut front, straight back and waistline gussets at each side. Open lower sleeves trimmed with galloon and gilt lace. Part of a Georgian Jewish woman's festive costume.
Silk, gilt thread, silk thread, galloon, cotton, length 125 cm, shoulder 38 cm, sleeve 48 cm
Transcaucasia - Eastern Georgia, 1900-1920s
From: Eastern Georgia, 1900-1920s
Transferred to the RME in 1939 from the Georgian Museum of Jewish History and Ethnography

132. 6397-20
Woman's tunic
Open at the front, with tapered sleeves, collar and edges trimmed with galloon.
Silk, galloon, length 136 cm, hem width 79 cm, sleeve 59 cm
Transcaucasia - Akhaltsikh, 1900-1920s
From: Georgia, Akhaltsikh, 1900-1920s
Transferred to the RME in 1939 from the Georgian Museum of Jewish History and Ethnography

133. 6397-22
Shawl
Rectangular green cloth with floral pattern and tassels.
Silk, 158 x 144 cm
Transcaucasia, 1900-1920s
From: Eastern Georgia, 1900-1920s
Transferred to the RME in 1939 from the Georgian Museum of Jewish History and Ethnography

134. 6397-27
Festive tablecloth
Rectangular dark brown cloth with floral pattern.
Silk, gilt thread, embroidery, 95 x 90 cm
Georgia, Tbilisi, 1900-1920s
From: Georgia, Tbilisi, 1900-1920s
Transferred to the RME in 1939 from the Georgian Museum of Jewish History and Ethnography

135. 6397-28
Bowl
Flat, bathing bowl with low sides, formed part of bride's dowry.
Tin-plated bronze, chiselled, chased, diam. bottom 19 cm, height 8 cm
Transcaucasia, late 18th - early 19th century
From: Georgia, late 18th - early 20th century
Transferred to the RME in 1939 from the Georgian Museum of Jewish History and Ethnography

136. 6397-29/ab
Snuffbox
Oval box with cover.
Carved wood, diam. 5,5 x 4 cm, height 7.5 cm
Georgia, 1900-1920s
From: Georgia, 1900-1920s
Transferred to the RME in 1939 from the Georgian Museum of Jewish History and Ethnography

137. 6397-30
Synagogue charity box
Semi-cylindrical box with flat back, an incision in the top and a lock. Hebrew inscription indicating collection before Passover to ensure a supply of flour for *mazzot* for the poor.
Painted tin, iron, diam. bottom 10 cm, height 19 cm
Georgia, 1880-1900s
From: Georgia, 1880-1920s
Transferred to the RME in 1939 from the Georgian Museum of Jewish History and Ethnography

138. 8761-5637
Candlestick
Wide base; for ritual use.
Copper, engraved, diam. bottom 10.5 cm, height 15 cm
Eastern Georgia, 1880-1900s
From: Eastern Georgia, Kareli, 1880-1920s
Purchased in 1929 by M.S. Plisetsky for the Moscow Museum of Ethnic Studies; transferred to the RME in 1948

139. 8761-5638
Mortar
Cylindrical vessel with central grip.
Wood, height 18 cm, diam. 13 cm
Western Georgia, Kutaisi, 1900-1920s
From: Western Georgia, Kutaisi, 1900-1920s
Purchased in 1929 by M.S. Plisetsky for the Moscow Museum of Ethnic Studies; transferred to the RME in 1948

140. 8761-5639
Bowl
Turned wood, height 7 cm, diam. 34 cm
Western Georgia, Kutaisi, 1900-1920s
From: Western Georgia, Kutaisi, 1900-1920s
Purchased in 1929 by M.S. Plisetsky for the Moscow Museum of Ethnic Studies; transferred to the RME in 1948

141. 8761-5640
Bowl
Bowl for dairy products.
Turned wood, height 5 cm, diam. 18 cm
Western Georgia, Kutaisi, 1900-1920s
From: Western Georgia, Kutaisi, 1900-1920s
Purchased in 1929 by M.S. Plisetsky for the Moscow Museum of Ethnic Studies; transferred to the RME in 1948

142. 8761-5641
Scoop
Square, short handle.
Carved wood, 26.5 x 23 cm
Western Georgia, Tskhinvali, 1900-1920s
From: Western Georgia, Tskhinvali, 1900-1920s
Purchased in 1929 by M.S. Plisetsky for the Moscow Museum of Ethnic Studies; transferred to the RME in 1948

143. 8761-5642
Ladle
Carved wood, 36 x 7 cm
Georgia, 1920s
From: Georgia, 1920s
Purchased in 1929 by M.S. Plisetsky for the Moscow Museum of Ethnic Studies; transferred to the RME in 1948

144. 8761-5643
Jar
With elongated neck, single handle and curved ornament.
Unglazed earthenware, height 29 cm, diam. 18 cm
Georgia, Shroshi, 1900-1920s
From: Georgia, 1900-1920s
Purchased in 1929 by M.S. Plisetsky for the Moscow Museum of Ethnic Studies; transferred to the RME in 1948

145. 8761-5644
Vessel
Single handle, wide mouth.
Ceramics, moulding, height 16 cm, diam. 16 cm
Georgia, 1900-1920s
From: Georgia, 1900-1920s
Purchased in 1929 by M.S. Plisetsky for the Moscow Museum of Ethnic Studies; transferred to the RME in 1948

146. 8761-5645
Pot
Glazed earthenware, painted under glazing with vine motif, height 16 cm, diam. 10 cm
Eastern Georgia, Gori (?) 1900-1920s
From: Georgia, 1900-1920s
Purchased in 1929 by M.S. Plisetsky for the Moscow Museum of Ethnic Studies; transferred to the RME in 1948

147. 8761-5646
Pitcher
Flat-bottomed pitcher with single handle, high neck and spout.
Tin-plated copper, chiselled, height 23 cm, diam. bottom 15 cm
Georgia, 1880-1920s
From: Georgia, 1880-1920s
Purchased in 1929 by M.S. Plisetsky for the Moscow Museum of Ethnic Studies; transferred to the RME in 1948

148. 8761-5647
Pitcher
Tin-plated copper, chiselled, height 33 cm, diam. bottom 21 cm
Georgia, 1880-1920s
From: Georgia, 18801920s
Purchased in 1929 by M.S. Plisetsky for the Moscow Museum of Ethnic Studies; transferred to the RME in 1948

149. 8761-5648
Pot
Cylindrical pot with handle.
Copper, chiselled, with iron handle, height 14 cm, diam. bottom 22 cm
Georgia, 1880-1920s
From: Georgia-1880-1920s
Purchased in 1929 by M.S. Plisetsky for the Moscow Museum of Ethnic Studies; transferred to the RME in 1948

150. 8761-5649
Spatula
Carved wood, 51 x 13 cm
Georgia, 1920s
From: Georgia, 1920s
Purchased in 1929 by M.S. Plisetsky for the Moscow Museum of Ethnic Studies; transferred to the RME in 1948

151. 8761-5652
Manuscript scroll
Book of Esther, read at Purim.
Parchment, wood, roller 26 cm, parchment width 11.5 cm
Palestine, early 20th century
From: Georgia, 1900-1920s
Purchased in 1929 by M.S. Plisetsky for the Moscow Museum of Ethnic Studies; transferred to the RME in 1948

152. 8761-5660
Saz
Plucked instrument with oval body and mother-of-pearl decoration on neck.
Wood, bone, horn, metal, mother of pearl, 63 x 12 cm
Transcaucasia, 1900-1920s
From: Georgia, 1900-1920s
Purchased in 1929 by M.S. Plisetsky for the Moscow Museum of Ethnic Studies; transferred to the RME in 1948

153. 8761-5662
Saz
Plucked instrument with oval body and mother-of-pearl decoration on neck.
Wood, bone, horn, metal, mother of pearl, 68 x 11.5 cm
Transcaucasia, 1900-1920s
From: Georgia, 1900-1920s.
Purchased in 1929 by M.S.Plisetsky for the Moscow Museum of Ethnic Studies; transferred to the RME in 1948

154. 8761-5663
Kamancha
Bowed instrument with circular body and mother-of-pearl decoration. Held vertical when played.
Wood, mother-of-pearl, bone, iron, 86 x 19 cm
Transcaucasia, 1900-1920s
From: Georgia, 1900-1920s
Purchased in 1929 by M.S. Plisetsky for the Moscow Museum of Ethnic Studies; transferred to the RME in 1948

155. 8761-5664
Tari
Plucked instrument with carved, oval body and short neck.
Wood, 59 x 19 cm
Transcaucasia, 1900-1920s
From: Georgia, 1900-1920s
Purchased in 1929 by M.S. Plisetsky for the Moscow Museum of Ethnic Studies; transferred to the RME in 1948

156. 8761-5666
Drum
Perforated cylinder with animal-skin drumhead held with straps.
Wood, leather, height 31 cm, diam. 30 cm
Transcaucasia, 1900-1920s
From: Georgia, 1900-1920s
Purchased in 1929 by M.S. Plisetsky for the Moscow Museum of Ethnic Studies; transferred to the RME in 1948

157. 8761-5667
Tari
Plucked instrument with oval body and short neck.
Wood, carving, 95 x 18 cm
Transcaucasia, 1900-1920s
From: Georgia, 1900-1920s
Purchased in 1929 by M.S. Plisetsky for the Moscow Museum of Ethnic Studies; transferred to the RME in 1948

158. 8762-13804
Man's trousers
Typical Caucasian trousers with long tapered legs with straps and two narrow gussets at the crutch.
Cotton, length 100 cm, waist 56 cm
Georgia, 1910-1920s
From: Georgia, 1910-1920s
Purchased in 1929 by M.S. Plisetsky for the Moscow Museum of Ethnic Studies; transferred to the RME in 1948

159. 8762-13812/1,2
Man's footwear
Traditional type of man's footwear with soft sole.
Leather, 27 x 15 cm
Georgia, 1910-1920s
From: Georgia, 1910-1920s
Purchased in 1929 by M.S. Plisetsky for the Moscow Museum of Ethnic Studies; transferred to the RME in 1948

160. 8762-13820
Hairpiece
Ornamental braid attached to women's headgear.
Hair, length 55 cm, diam. 4 cm
Western Georgia, 1900-1920s
From: Western Georgia, Kutaisi, 1900-1920s
Purchased in 1929 by M.S. Plisetsky for the Moscow Museum of Ethnic Studies; transferred to the RME in 1948

161. 8762-13821
Hairpiece
Two locks of hair linked with ribbon, worn at the temples and attached to headgear. Probably derived from hairpieces traditionally worn by married Jewish women.
Hair, cotton, 15 x 9 cm
Georgia, 1900-1920s
From: Western Georgia, Kutaisi, 1900-1920s
Purchased in 1929 by M.S. Plisetsky for the Moscow Museum of Ethnic Studies; transferred to the RME in 1948

162. 8762-13822
Necklace
String of 28 beads.
Amber, glass, 46 cm
Georgia, 19th century
From: Georgia, 1900-1920s
Purchased in 1929 by M.S. Plisetsky for the Moscow Museum of Ethnic Studies; transferred to the RME in 1948

163-167.
Crib set
The crib cover was probably manufactured in the 1920s or earlier and was used continually. The other objects were made and used in the year they were purchased for the museum.
Western Georgia, Kutaisi
Purchased in 1929 by M.S. Plisetsky for the Moscow Museum of Ethnic Studies; transferred to the RME in 1948

163. 8762-13830
Crib cover
A crib cover to protect the child from direct sunlight and flies.
Sateen, 92 x 49 cm

164. 8762-13831
Sheet
Cotton, 65 x 57 cm

165. 8762-13832
Sheet
The hole in the sheet is for a urine tube.
Cotton, 42 x 35 cm

166. 8762-13833
Sheet
The hole in the sheet is for a urine tube.
Cotton, 97 x 75 cm

167. 8762-13834
Binder
A cloth for securing the baby in the crib.
Cotton, 94 x 15 cm

168. 8762-13835
Mila
Boy's amulet with two bags, the larger containing the boy's foreskin.
Cotton, leather, band 100 x 1 cm
Western Georgia, Racha, Sakhcheri village, 1929-1930s
From: Western Georgia, Racha, Sakhcheri village, 1929-1930s
Purchased in 1930 by M.S. Plisetsky for the Moscow Museum of Ethnic Studies; transferred to the RME in 1948

169. 8762-13838
Nukhsa
Boy's amulet bag with four triangular pieces of cloth (two yellow, two mauve), stitched to form an envelope with a central button and sewn onto the coat to protect against epilepsy. Given to the collector by the father secretly, without his wife's consent.
Cotton, 8.5 x 8 cm
Georgia, Akhaltsikh, 1928-1930
From: Georgia, Akhaltsikh, Isaac Beshiashvili's family, 1928-1930
Purchased in 1930 by M.S. Plisetsky for the Moscow Museum of Ethnic Studies; transferred to the RME in 1948

170. 8762-13839
Nukhsa
Amulet for a baby boy with an envelope-shaped bag containing a piece of paper with random Arabic and Hebrew letters written in an unskilled hand with child's drawings, sewn on a garment, generally on the back, to protect against evil spirits.
Brocade, paper, bag 8.5 x 8 cm, paper 44.5 x 19.5 cm
Georgia, Akhaltsikh, 1928-1930s
From: Georgia, Akhaltsikh, 1928-1930s
Purchased in 1930 by M.S. Plisetsky for the Moscow Museum of Ethnic Studies; transferred to the RME in 1948

171. 8762-13840
Amulet
Rectangular cloth with four circles containing Arabic inscriptions in Indian ink and a rectangular cartouche in the lower left corner containing a crowned figure with a magic table forming the torso.
Cotton, 39 x 12.5 cm
Transcaucasia, 19th century
From: Georgia, early 20th century
Purchased in 1930 by M.S. Plisetsky for the Moscow Museum of Ethnic Studies; transferred to the RME in 1948

172. 8762-13841
Amulet
Rectangular plaque with loop containing a piece of paper with Hebrew inscriptions and a central *Magen David* around the word Jerusalem and surrounded by the names of angels and names for God with an abbreviation for prosperity and wealth to be hung as an amulet in the house.
Iron, glass, paper, 8 x 6 cm
Palestine, late 19th century
From: Georgia, late 19th - early 20th century
Purchased probably in 1929-1930 by M.S. Plisetsky for the Moscow Museum of Ethnic Studies; transferred to the RME in 1948

173. 8762-13842
Ornament
Upholstered cardboard circles, possibly an amulet.
Cardboard, velvet, silk, 18 x 11 cm
Georgia, 1900-1920s
From: Georgia, 1900-1920s
Purchased probably in 1929-1930 by M.S. Plisetsky for the Moscow Museum of Ethnic Studies; transferred to the RME in 1948

174. 8761-15730
Plate
Yiddish inscription 'Bread, meat and fish are a joy at table'.
Ceramic, moulded, height 4 cm, diam. 26 cm
Bohemia (?), late 19th-early 20th century
From: Georgia, Tbilisi, 1880-1920s
Purchased probably in 1929-1930 by M.S. Plisetsky for the Moscow Museum of Ethnic Studies; transferred to the RME in 1948

175. 8762-33440
Amulet
Bag containing two pieces of paper with tables containing dashes in the cells.
Leather, paper, straps 35 x 5 cm, bag 5 x 4 cm
Georgia, late 19th - early 20th century
From: Georgia, late 19th century - 1920s
Purchased in 1930 by M.S. Plisetsky for the Moscow Museum of Ethnic Studies; transferred to the RME in 1948

176. 8385-1
Woman's tunic
Open down to the waist at the front and fastened with buttons, this typical Caucasian garment has gussets at the sides, straight sleeves with tight cuffs, the edges trimmed with galloon.
Silk, galloon, length 117 cm, shoulder 54 cm, sleeve 46 cm
Georgia, Akhaltsikh, second half of 19th century
From: Georgia, Akhaltsikh, second half of 19th century - 1910s
Purchased in 1974 in St Petersburg from a private owner

177. 8385-4
Woman's dress
Open front, straight back with tight waist, gussets at the sides, with three string buttons above the waist; long straight sleeves with slits and cuffs, trimmed with ribbon and lace.
Silk, cotton, cotton thread, silk thread, length 127 cm, shoulder 49 cm, sleeve 70 cm
Georgia, Akhaltsikh, mid 19th century
From: Georgia, Akhaltsikh, late 19th - early 20th century
Purchased in 1974 in St Petersburg from a private owner

178. 8385-6ab
Woman's blouse and skirt
Urban version of a traditional costume featuring an open blouse with a tight waist, basque, long, wide sleeves, and folds from the shoulder, trimmed with galloon and fastened at the front with hooks; the skirt with fine pleats, fastened with a hook at the side.
Silk, galloon, cotton, blouse: length 64 cm, shoulder 40 cm, sleeve 53 cm, skirt: length 95 cm, waist 70 cm, width hem 325 cm
Georgia, Akhaltsikh, early 20th century
From: Georgia, Akhaltsikh, 1910-1930s
Purchased in 1974 in St Petersburg from a private owner

179. 8385-13
Scarf
White cloth with floral pattern worn by girls on open braided hair with corners hanging loose in front and worn by women over two shawls, one with ends tied under the chin and at the back, the other arranged as a band around the forehead.
Finely woven silk, 241 x 72 cm
Georgia, Akhaltsikh, late 19th century
From: Georgia, Akhaltsikh, late 19th - early 20th century
Purchased in 1974 in St Petersburg from a private owner

180. 8385-14
Scarf
White scarf with floral pattern worn by girls on open braided hair with corners hanging loose in front and worn by women over two shawls, one with ends tied under the chin and at the back, the other arranged as a band around the forehead.
Finely woven silk, 213 x 73 cm
Georgia, Akhaltsikh, late 19th century
From: Georgia, Akhaltsikh, late 19th - early 20th century
Purchased in 1974 in St Petersburg from a private owner

181. 8385-17
Woman's tunic
Typical Caucasian cut with straight sleeves, open front to the waist, gathered at the shoulder near the collar with side gussets and a single button fastener.
Silk, cotton, gold thread, galloon, filigree

button, gilt metal, length 131 cm, shoulder 54 cm, sleeve 58 cm
Georgia, Akhaltsikh, late 19th century
From: Georgia, Akhaltsikh, late 19th - early 20th century
Purchased in 1974 in St Petersburg from a private owner

182. 8385-18
Woman's breeches
Wide model with tapered legs.
Silk, rep, Oriental cloth, length 76 cm, waist 76 cm
Georgia, Akhaltsikh, late 19th century
From: Georgia, Akhaltsikh, late 19th - early 20th century
Purchased in 1974 in St Petersburg from a private owner

183. 8385-19
Wedding dress
Known as a 'golden dress', this unique garment was given to the collector secretly by the donor, without his wife's consent. Open, straight front and back, with tight waist, gussets at the sides, a single button fastener at the waist, a shoulder seam and trimmed with galloon; straight sleeves, open from the elbow.
Brocade, silk, cotton, gilt thread, length 137 cm, shoulder 39 cm, sleeve 70 cm
Georgia, Akhaltsikh, second half of 19th century
From: Georgia, Akhaltsikh, late 19th - early 20th century
Purchased in 1974 in St Petersburg from a private owner

184. 8385-20
Woman's coat
This festive garment was worn by a wealthy urban woman in Transcaucasia. Open, tight at the waist with front flaps, fine pleats, sides and back, at the waist; long sleeves open at the end with cuffs, and fine folds in the upper sleeve, trimmed with fur and lined with cotton.
Silk, velvet, cotton, fur, ribbon, length 107 cm, shoulder 34 cm, sleeve 89 cm
Georgia, Akhaltsikh, late 19th century
From: Georgia, Akhaltsikh, late 19th - early 20th century
Purchased in 1974 in St Petersburg from a private contributor

185. 8385-21
Shawl
Tulle, silk, application on tulle, 308 x 143 cm
Georgia, Akhaltsikh, late 19th - early 20th century
From: Georgia, Akhaltsikh, late 19th - early 20th century
Purchased in 1974 in St Petersburg from a private owner

186. 8385-22
Man's bathrobe
Straight open robe with hood, wide elbow-length sleeves trimmed with fringe. Customs stamp on the front bottom section, acquired in Turkey by the bride's father as part of the dowry and given to the bridegroom.
Cotton, length 127 cm, shoulder 89 cm, sleeve 33 cm
Turkey, late 19th century
From: Georgia, Akhaltsikh, late 19th - early 20th century
Purchased in 1974 in St Petersburg from a private owner

187. 8385-34
Embroidery
Typical urban artefact.
Cotton, silk thread, chain-stitched, 68 x 48 cm
Georgia, Akhaltsikh, late 19th century
From: Georgia, Akhaltsikh, late 19th - early 20th century
Purchased in 1974 in St Petersburg from a private owner

188. 8385-37
Cloth
Central piece with printed Hebrew text surrounded by bands of coloured pieces. Central section features an heraldic design flanked by lions with inscription above a seven-branched Menorah and religious objects, with on either side pictures of the holy sites in Palestine. To the right and left, Hebrew texts for the Sabbath. Marked with the stamp of Halevi Zukkerman printing works in Jerusalem and dated 1914, the cloth was assembled in Georgia, Akhaltsikh in 1914-1915. Its final shape is reminiscent of the *bokhcha* napkins used for carrying small articles. Known locally as a *mizrah-supra*, the second part is a local Georgian term for tablecloth, the first part, *mizrah*, refers to an ornament for the wall facing Jerusalem.
Central print: cotton, print, Palestine, Jerusalem 1914
Margins: silk, cotton, made of 4-5 pieces of Turkish coloured cloth, total size 60 x 60 cm
Georgia, Akhaltsikh, 1914-1915
From: Georgia, Akhaltsikh, 1915-1930s
Purchased in 1974 in St Petersburg from a private owner

189. 8385-45
Sugar cone cover
Gold-embroidered cloth to cover a plate of sweets (brought by the groom to the bride's house as symbol of the parent's consent to the match).
Cotton, gold thread, cotton thread, 72 (sewn together) x 69 cm
Georgia, Akhaltsikh, late 19th - early 20th century
From: Georgia, Akhaltsikh, late 19th - early 20th century
Purchased in 1974 in St Petersburg from a private owner

190. 1005-HB
Replica loaf of bread
Plaster, diam. 9.5 cm
Georgia

191. 1006-HB
Replica loaf of bread
Plaster, diam. 22 cm
Georgia

192. 1007-HB
Replica loaf of bread
Plaster, diam. 31.5 cm
Georgia

193. 0-1897-HB
Hebrew manuscript
Manual for amulets and spells, written on assorted pieces of paper by various scribes in diffrent Hebrew scripts. One of the texts is dated 1916.
Cardboard, paper, Indian ink, 22 x 17 cm
From: Georgia, second half of 1910s

Vladimir Dmitriev

GLOSSARY

The following list offers brief explanations of various terms used in the text.

aliyah *emigration to Israel*
Aron ha-kodesh *Holy Ark in synagogue for Torah scrolls (Ashkenazic)*
atsei hayyim *Torah scroll rollers*

bar mitzvah *coming of age ceremony for Jewish boys*
bimah *platform from which the Torah is read (Ashkenazic)*

hadas *spicebox*
hakham *chief rabbi*
Hanukkia, pl Hanukkiot *Hanukkah lamp*
havdalah *ceremony for the end of Sabbath*
hazzan *cantor*
heder *Jewish elementary school*
Hekhal *Holy Ark in synagogue for Torah scrolls (Sephardic)*
Hoshana Rabba *Seventh day of Sukkot*

kashrut *dietary regulations*
keter Torah *Crown of Torah*
kiddush cup *ritual wine goblet*

lulav *palm branch, one of four plants for Sukkot*

mazzah, pl. mazzot *unleavened bread for Passover*
melamed *teacher*
menorah *seven-branched candelabrum*
mezuzah *small container on the doorpost, with parchment*
mikveh *ritual bath*
minyan *quorum of ten men required for full religious service*
Mishneh Torah *legal code written by Maimonides (1135-1204)*
mizrah *(lit. East) plaque on the wall to indicate the direction of Jerusalem, for prayer*
mohel *circumciser*

parokhet pl. parokhot *curtain to cover the Holy Ark*
Pesah *Passover*
piyyutim *liturgical poems*
Purim *Feast of Lots*

responsa *answers to religious questions*
rimmonim *Torah scroll finials*

Seder plate *plate for the Passover meal*
shammash *beadle*
Shavuot *Feast of Weeks*
shehitah *ritual slaughtering*
Shemoneh Esreh *the main statutory prayer containing a series of benedictions*
shivviti *decorative plaque with a verse from Psalm 16:8*
shofar *horn used on the High Holidays*
shohet *ritual slaughterer*
sukkah *booth, tabernacle*
Sukkot *Festival of Tabernacles*

tallit *prayershawl*
tallit katan *fringed ritual undergarment*
tefillin *phylacteries*
tevah *platform from which the Torah is read (Sephardic)*

yad *pointer for reading from the Torah*
yeshiva *religious academy*
Yom Kippur *Day of Atonement*

zizit *prayershawl fringes*

INDEX CATALOGUE

Central Asia

Amulets
  Chordevoli 14, 15, 17
  Komsa 10, 11, 12, 13
  Mioro 16
Clothing, men
  Belt 22
  Boots 25
  Gown 62
  Hat 1, 23, 26
  Outer gown 21
  Skull cap 2, 24
  Under gown 20
Clothing, women
  Cap 53
  Dress 38, 39, 41, 42, 43, 44, 45, 46, 47, 48
  Gown 49, 50
  Kulutapushak 29, 30, 31, 32, 33, 52
  Munisak 3
  Paranja 51
  Peshonaband 54, 55, 56
  Sarband 37
  Shawl 57, 58, 59, 60, 61
Household articles
  Bowl 66, 67
  Khum 74
  Ladle 68, 69
  Pestle and mortar 70
  Spiked mazzah rolling pin 75
  Tray 71, 72, 73
Jewellery
  Bracelet 35, 36, 64
  Earrings 65
  Nosi gardan 63
  Poncha 27
  Tavk 28
Religious objects
  Letter 19
  Mezuzah 9
  New Year greeting card 18
  Rimmonim 76
  Tallit 34
  Tallit katan (beged) 4
  Tefillin 5
  Tefillin bag 7, 8
  Tefillin cases 6
  Torah scroll case 40

Additional items Central Asia

Clothing, men
  Belt 106, 120
  Cap 128
  Kamzol 127
  Robe 105, 111
  Shirt 90
  Skull cap 113
Clothing, women
  Chachvan 77

Dress 80
Kerchief 78, 79, 81
Scarf 124
Shawl 123
Household articles
  Bowl 102, 103
  Cage-spool 100
  Candlestick 85, 95
  Carpet 86, 126
  Chest 104
  Cloth 82, 92
  Dish 98, 101
  Drinking cup 93, 96
  Jug 83, 84, 87, 114
  Piola 125
  Plate 122
  Printed fabric 91
  Rug 110
  Suzani 108, 109, 115
  Teapot 116
  Tray 99
  Vessel for ablution 119
  Vessel for water 89, 94
  Wash-stand 88
Jewellery
  Beads 117, 118
  Breast adornment 107
  Breast decoration 121
  Necklace 97, 112

Mountain Jews

Amulets 65, 66
  Geikhal 5
  Kash 2, 3, 4
  Talysim 6, 7, 8
Clothing, women
  Belt 31, 55
  Breeches 50
  Chargat 32
  Chukht 36, 54
  Costume 49-58
  Detachable sleeves 62
  Festive dress 51
  Footwear 53
  Hairpiece ornament 23
  Head ornament 22
  Headpiece 27
  Jacket 38
  Kalagai 34
  Shawl 35, 56, 57
  Socks, pair of 39, 52
  Tunic 33, 49
Household articles
  Board 43
  Child's toboggan 46
  Last 40
  Loom 45
  Namazlyk 61
  Rolling pin 42
  Spatula 41
  Spindle 44
  Pitcher 11
  Toy cradle 47

Tobacco pouch 63
Jewellery
  Bracelet 20, 29
  Brooch 24, 28
  Collar stud 59
  Earrings 30
  Necklace 16, 17, 21, 58
  Pendant 25, 26, 37
  Signet ring with cornelian 60
  String of beads 18, 19
Religious objects
  Hadas 48
  Havdalah candle 12
  Jaryk 9
  Mezuzah case 1
  Parde 64
  Rimmonim 14
  Ritual whip 15
  Shofar 10
  Torah pointers 13

Additional Tat items

Clothing, men
  Bashlyk 82b
  Belt 82f
  Boots 82g
  Breeches 82e
  Cherkess chokha 82d
  Pair of socks 69
  Papakha 82a, 83
  Shirt 82c
Household goods
  Bowl 91, 101
  Colander 105
  Crib 84
  Cup 93, 94, 95, 96
  Frying pan 107, 108
  Khaly 76, 77, 78
  Khaly gebe 79
  Khurjinn 73
  Mafrasj 72
  Milking pail 98, 99, 100
  Namazlyk 80
  Oil lamp 92
  Ornament 68
  Pillow case 74
  Pitcher 97
  Pot with lid 104
  Printed design 71
  Rug 75
  Saddle blanket 67
  Saltcellar 81
  Skimmer 106
  Spoon 86, 87, 88, 89, 90
  Spoon holder 70
  Tray 102, 103
  Tripod 85
Map of Central Asia 109

Georgian Jews

Amulet 171, 172, 175
  Mila 168

  Nukhsa 169, 170
  Ornament 173
Clothing, men
  Arkhalukh 121, 123
  Bathrobe 186
  Footwear 159
  Trousers 158
  Waistcoat 122
  Rabbi's gown 124
Clothing, women
  Blouse and skirt 178
  Boots, pair of 118
  Breeches 120, 182
  Bridal costume 110-119
  Coat 184
  Dress 177
  Hairpiece 160, 161
  Mules, pair of 119
  Outer dress 131
  Outer kaptal 112
  Scarf 113, 114, 179, 180
  Shawl 133, 185
  Tunic 132, 176, 181
  Under kaptal 111
  Under tunic 110
  Veil 115
  Wedding dress 183
Household articles
  Binder 167
  Bowl 135, 140, 141
  Crib cover 163
  Crib set 163-167
  Drum 156
  Embroidery 187
  Festive tablecloth 134
  Jar 144
  Kamancha 154
  Ladle 143
  Mortar 129, 139
  Pitcher 147, 148
  Plate 174
  Pot 126, 146, 149
  Replica loaf of bread 190, 191, 192
  Saz 152, 153
  Scoop 142
  Sheet 164, 165, 166
  Snuffbox 136
  Spatula 150
  Spinning top 128
  Sugar cone cover 189
  Tari 155, 157
  Vessel 145
  Water jug 127
Jewellery
  Earrings 117
  Necklace 116, 162
Religious objects
  Candlestick 138
  Cloth 188
  Hebrew manuscript 193
  Manuscript scroll 151
  Shofar 125
  Spice box 130
  Synagogue charity box 137

ACKNOWLEDGEMENTS

Exhibition

IN RUSSIA

Project coordination
Ludmila Uritskaya

Exhibition curators
Vladimir Dmitriev
Tatjana Emelyanenko

Translations
S. Parizjsky, from Hebrew
G. Pluzjnikova, from Russian

INTERMEDIARY
Alla Geller, Holland Russia Trade Services

IN THE NETHERLANDS
Exhibition curator
Hetty Berg

Coordination
Bernadette van Woerkom

Translations
Sam Herman

Design
Monique Rietbroek

Graphic design
Marit van der Meer

Technical realisation
fa. Peeterse
Technical Department JHM

Catalogue
Editor
Hetty Berg

Deputy editor
Sam Herman

Copy editing
Mariëlla Beukers

Translations
A. Glebovskaya, Jewish University, St Petersburg, from Russian
W. Jac. van Bekkum, excerpts Pulner Archive, from Hebrew

Graphic design
Victor Levie

Photography
Frits Terpoorten

Print
Waanders Printers, Zwolle

Published by
Waanders Publishers, Zwolle

© Uitgeverij Waanders b.v., Zwolle
Russian Museum of Ethnography, St Petersburg
Joods Historisch Museum, Amsterdam

All rights reserved. No part of this publication may be reproduced or transmitted in any form or by any means, electronic or mechanical, including photocopy, recording or any other information storage and retrieval system, without prior permission in writing by the publisher.

ISBN 90 400 9216 8
NUGI 633, 641

Jewish woman wearing a hairpiece. (Beth Hatefutsoth Photo Archive, courtesy of S. Shvili, Jerusalem)

Cover
Family of Mountain Jews, Dagestan. Photo by D.I. Ermakov, 1878-1916. (Russian Museum of Ethnography)

Bridal costume, Akhaltsikh, Georgia (cat. nos 110-119)